No Further Harm

A Purely Predictable Path

Mark (Marcus) Mann

Access the Personal Risk Checklist
(myriskchecklist.com)

Copyright © 2019 Mark (Marcus) Mann

All rights reserved.

ISBN: 9780615625300

DEDICATION

To those impacted by senseless violence and tragic accidents.
Your courage and candor will not be forgotten.

CONTENTS

Acknowledgments, Suggested Use & Terminology

1	Predictable Harm on Costa Concordia	1
2	Safety: A Changing Culture	27
3	Victim Mindset: A Temporary Condition	45
4	Distraction and Vulnerability	65
5	Assumptions: A Wakeup Call	83
6	Core Concepts: Accelerating the Solution	101
7	Physical Property Assessment	123
8	Face-to-Face & De-escalation	143
9	The Active Shooter Profile	177
	Case Studies & Analysis	209
	About the Author	248
	Legal Disclaimer	249

ACKNOWLEDGMENTS

Washington State Transportation Insurance Pool (WSTIP) Data and Focus: Tracey Christianson, Joanne Kerrigan, Chris DeVoll, Laura Jewell, and Al Hatten (ret).

Roberto Lopez, Global Safety Advisor, Flatiron Corporation.

Joseph Chandler, Historical Context, Bayley Corporation.

Rebecca Llewellyn and Washington State Governor's Industrial Safety and Health Advisory Board

Visible Violence & Copycats, Joline Gutierrez Krueger, reprinted by permission from the Albuquerque Tribune.

Associated General Contractors (AGCWA) Data and Focus: Diane Kocer, Mandi Kime, Dan Morris and Staff.

Smart Safety Summit, Focus Group: Brian Ducey, Rhett Carpenter.

Bob Moawad & Ann Rule, Mentor, Author and Speaker.

Intelex EHSQ, Global Focus Group Online, Tamara Parris.

Gavin DeBecker, Author and Speaker, Terminology and Process: The Gift of Fear, Fearless.

1,300 More School Threats at U.S. Schools in 2017, Report Finds. Marina Pitofsky, USA Today.

Mark Panther, Public Safety & Community Leader, Mentor, Process, Reality, Validation.

Violent Plot Uncovered, U.S. Says, by Dan Eggen and Susan Schmidt, The Washington Post Company.

SUGGESTIONS: USE OF THE TEXT

The following recommendations may enhance the lessons offered in the text. To support the idea that knowledge used is better remembered, action is recommended as you conclude each section. This is the first nonfiction addressing the reduction of both violence and accidental harm as a package. Finding and describing common human traits was not easy, and one or two lessons in this text may be equally difficult to grasp. The educational value expands when two or more individuals move these concepts into practice. The journey is more enjoyable when it includes small groups, or teams found in your current school, church, workplace, community, and home.

No Further Harm, imitative of the famous oath coined by Greek Physician Hippocrates, was launched in the mind years before this text. Primum non nocere calls on everyone, not just the medical community, to protect without creating a path of destruction. The method is a direct result of research supporting prevention, live application when facing a threat, and a process to evaluate unfortunate events after the fact. Respect-Respond-Review suggests we safeguard people, places, and things by: Respecting five dimensions of predictable harm Respond within the framework of twelve core concepts and Review past hurts by answering five helpful questions.

Performance science is a changing discipline, forecasting being one of the components. Like everything new, forecasting must survive your scrutiny by suffering the natural stages of denial, rejection, assimilation, and hopefully, gradual acceptance. I previously denied injuries and acts were predictable, rejecting spontaneous harm as foreseeable. I saw the light through my own experience as witness, investigator, and the drama of a brush with death. The book accommodates those who prefer to learn without unnecessary pain through the experience of others. Improvement areas outlined in the text include four basic opinions:

1. While predicting harm is a preventative action, it calls for the detailed examination of past acts, incidents, and accidents. How we evaluate recent casualties, specifically victims, affect the future of safety.

2. Evidence shows we are suffering from competing values. The rapid communication necessary for preventing harm is in collision with hypersensitivity and the fear of offending others.

3. Our intuitive sense to recognize a threat has been compromised by distractions. The full-time flow of data and related interruptions is now a key contributor to serious injury and premature death. Irrefutable evidence will support the theory.

4. Visible accidents and humanmade tragedies are often blamed erroneously on process and equipment. With natural disasters being the only exception, Human factors have stepped up as a formidable threat to safety.

The demographics for this text and topic suggest you are most likely a professional, possibly a strategist, and the informed teacher, parent, and responsible community member. Those who care about others significantly influence the safety of all; exercising leadership and teaching enhanced awareness are compelling skills. Therefore, this book includes sobering tips for educating peers, family, students, and co-workers in risk-reduction. Intentionally arranged in brief and actionable sections, the blend intends to affect the greatest number of adult learning styles. Case studies include details and factual conclusions; victims and others affirm the twelve concepts described in chapter six.

I encourage you to suspend the popular notion of a solo-cause and solo-cure for violence and accidents. Those who believe they have the only answer for cause or cure may be frustrated by this text, which offers many possibilities. In addition to content, my job is to help organize thoughts and present a menu of options. The written product follows the live format of presentations and webinar format, avoiding unnecessary topics that split the audience. The single-cause, solo-solution approach to personal or workplace safety has failed. The best platform expands the prevention footprint, minus distractions. While I have strong opinions on many world events, the text focuses on those supporting the theme. Ending mass violence, school shootings, and catastrophic accidents call for a full-court press, all parties, all backgrounds, and all-hands on-topic, minus misplaced activism.

The text does not replace policy, procedures, and law; however, our goal is to enhance the entire landscape. I encourage students and readers to be smart, be observant, be deliberate, and be fearless. Amazing things will happen as you consider any act or accident through educational filter and continue the crucial conversation.

Thank you for your interest and the respect you have for others and yourself. By working together, moving beyond blind anger and blame, a growing culture of solutions is within reach.

Chapter Summary

Chapter one introduces the topic and captures lessons-learned from the 2012 sinking of the Costa Concordia Cruise liner, lost in the Mediterranean Sea. The section also suggests five questions leading to the necessary lessons after any injury or act.

Chapter two is dedicated to the everchanging safety culture; capturing new lessons as each occurrence unfolds, and suggestions leading to constant and never-ending improvement

Chapter three will refresh the controversial topic of victim thinking and its influence; however, our discussion tags a temporary attitude over a fixed victim personality.

Chapter four provides evidence of dangerous distractions and suggests a few solutions based on real-world incidents and accidents.

Chapter five touches on the big wakeup call many have experienced and leading to essential life-changes. This the chapter for survivors, those empowered by a victim experience.

Chapter six includes core concepts supporting the art and science that hone skills needed for predicting and preventing harm.

Chapter seven addresses an unusual topic we rarely consider. Our safe habits are challenged by all-things-new, including a home, new workspace, and the special conference or vacation destination.

Chapter eight dives into the most dangerous, challenging, and arguably most crucial exercise outlined in the book. Assessing a human risk face-to-face and gathering lifesaving clues.

Chapter nine is a must-read as the FBI shares a profile of the Active Shooter, which includes remarkable insight and lessons.

Case studies complete the text with the analysis of actual incidents and accidents. The concluding section includes examples and the application of our five strategic questions.

Terms & Vocabulary

The text relies on both traditional verbiage, essential terms, and a language that may be unfamiliar. In the practice of prevention, common language minimizes the need to describe every risk in detail. Frequently used terms include:

Act:

What we do, should be doing, and what we may have missed related to intentional harm, accidental injury, and a near miss.

Assault:

Intentional acts, unwanted contact of any kind that may harm or threaten another person physically, via harassment, and all intimidation, implied, written and meeting the legal threshold beyond a policy violation.

Harassment:

Any offensive and intentional conduct based on age, disability, medical condition, domestic circumstances, gender, sexual orientation, race, color, language, religion, political affiliation, trade union, national or social origin, and is unwanted. Harassment includes behavior or words affecting dignity at work, public meetings, schools, and areas of worship. Harassment need not reach the threshold of criminal behavior to be considered an environmental clue of predictable harm.

Near Miss:

Any situation, fact, or combination of circumstances where harm would have likely occurred but did not end in injury or physical property damage. Examples may include stepping into traffic while skimming social media and experiencing a near miss with a moving vehicle. A near miss may include traversing an active construction site without the needed awareness and experiencing a close call with equipment or a new hazard. We highlight the near miss as an opportunity to learn and teach others. The near miss is more frequent than actual harm but often overlooked; a chance to improve safety without the trauma.

Offender:

Any person who commits an act of violence, threatens, engages in a plan to harm, or becomes the subject of concern based on behavior described in this text. The book uses the term when the average human becomes a target of interest, or otherwise earns the dubious tag through clues, cues, and defined risk. If the section or chapter refers to a person as an offender, the subject is near or beyond the threshold of predictable harm. "Offender" tags the individual as a potential threat.

Threat:

This text uses the term in two slightly different applications: (A) individual behavior, and (B) specific environment:

(A) Implied intent to use physical force or illicit power and the implication results in fear of physical, fiscal, or adverse consequences to individual or group. The threat includes implied consequences leading to fear, danger, or a reasonable concern the words or communicated threat could lead to actual harm, or

(B) The environment, conditions, and conclusion presented by the evidence, a reasonable assumption, or systematic forecast of risk.

Victim:

Any person, group or organization directly or indirectly affected by an act of violence. This includes behavior described above, and any action or omission leading to harm, occupational injury, near-miss, or fatality.

Workplace:

Any facility, sublet, satellite location, temporary worksite, meeting location of two or more employees, including all related parking areas. Regardless of size, workplace includes any situation where work-related services are being planned, performed, discussed and evaluated.

No Further Harm: A Purely Predictable Path

CHAPTER ONE:

Predictable Harm on Costa Concordia

The first images were surprising and surreal; like a framed portrait, the Mediterranean Sea in full glorious sunshine, and a quaint nearby island community known as Isola del Giglio. A fifteen-story structure was awkwardly and dangerously leaning toward the island. It was Lady Concordia, and she was horribly injured. Previously a proud mammoth, she had rolled onto her side, seemingly a sign of surrender. Bragging 1500 cabins, adorned with fresh cut flowers and surrounded by polished brass, she was no longer the model of health. The eight-year-old ship was dying. The assembly included beautiful glass, the world's largest spa-at-sea, and four level swimming pools 48-hours earlier. Costa Concordia would be remembered for her five

restaurants, thirteen bars, a casino, young dancers, and a slightly older crew in fitted tuxedos. This beautiful ship packaged with swag and carved ice, did not line up with a horrible story and brutal accusations directed toward her

handlers. She had been changed forever; terror and multiple fatalities now associated with her dubious name.

The scene would become one of many I visited live and virtually as I researched cases for this book and project, entitled No Further Harm. Eventually, I asked those close to the Mediterranean tragedy five questions about the shipwreck, the same inquiry I've sought and highly recommend in all tragic events, big or small. They offer a starting point for any related conversation; the opportunity to extract helpful lessons after any unfortunate incident you happen upon live or via media:

1. **Was it predictable?**
2. **What was the distraction?**
3. **Does it call for conversation, intervention or penalty?**
4. **Is the cause trending?**
5. **What is the teachable resolution or short-term fix?**

We often sidestep the discussion around violence, catastrophic events, and common accidents caused by less-than-perfect humans. Much of the general ugliness in the world is predictable, tragic outcomes and premature mortality avoidable. In many cases, we delay the meaningful conversation. Our failure to look beyond a single theory morphs into a mistaken conclusion that a closer look is not necessary. The horrific crisis involving the Costa Concordia cruise ship was not an exception to the rule.

I've examined many cases in preparing this text; some meeting the needed threshold for publication, many did not. Others met a hard edge in the simplicity of cause. The breach of duty is widespread; poor outcomes due to an oversight; a capable soul had information that could have prevented the loss and failed, forgot, or refused to share the data.

We usually don't want to discuss the human mistakes leading to a crisis. Caught up in the emotion of mass violence, a transit or construction accident, and after a school shooting, mining for patterns of human error are not the first concern. Many don't have the interest or ability, and safety officers may not have the permission to pursue common denominators found in the pattern of human error. We blame equipment, weather, and training; easier to swallow and a more comfortable discussion. Those who dodge this crucial conversation are no longer a small group. They are far from alone in their discomfort; most humans prefer to blame a massive force, an unforeseen hazard, a flawed policy, and the global conditions for a simple human mistake. Unfortunately, the anything-but-me conversation is often misdirected, the compassionate attempt to avoid judgment of our peers, employers and loved ones. May I be the first to proclaim my guilt.

Odd as it may be, forecasting casualties is part of my job. I independently predict success and failure, so we can pursue the best by avoiding the ugly stuff. The role is unusual; a unique performance science considered a practice rather than a policy. Forecasting harm is a skill rather than a job, and I try to do it in all parts of my life. My business name reflects my passion, 'my favorites' file holds the evidence, and my peer group has the same appetite. The work is interesting, packed with lessons, and heartbreaking at times. Predictable casualties take a toll on everyone; increasingly painful for those in the safety and teaching professions.

Predictability is a beautiful option. Predictions usually precede our performance. Safety, success, and healthy habits begin with a conscious and deliberate forecast, also called an estimation or goal. The conversation behind the scenes has become more colorful recently, exploding as a series of preventable acts, accidents, and deaths broke many records. I've been nudged to share ideas in this text and encouraged to expand the prevention-footprint. I believe in giving cues and the clues of likely harm the less-than-ambiguous distinction of teachable moments. This chapter will introduce the basics related to Environmental Forecasting; recognizing dangerous conditions with time to spare and room to respond. The journey thru the stages is challenging but doable; relying on natural skills you have had since birth, and a gift some have allowed to drowse-off.

Judgment, a human skill often cursed by my progressive friends, and misunderstood or abused by others, is not an obscenity or moral value we should hide. Our ability to move safely and confidently through our day, to predict and avoid harm is overdue for periodic maintenance. The lessons buried below the surface of our predictable losses need courageous exposure, depth, and the awakening of our intuitive analysis of people, places, and things. The cultural collision will continue until we care enough to judge, place sensitivities on hold, and unleash lifesaving observations. The frightening and factual danger before us includes a boisterous silence.

The exercise in judgment is a daily challenge. Working out the choice, an ability to differentiate, has become a daily decision. The recent evidence clearly says we will choose to live comfortably, be painfully injured, or ignore the lifesaving decision and throw the dice. Rarely a pleasant dinner chat, this book will discuss judgment; assessing those within our circle of influence and explaining our observations promptly when proper or possible.

It seems judgment was tossed out of the adult conversation in recent years, cursed by misunderstanding, and replaced with something softer on the palate. Flawed judgment and avoidance are in the chain-of-events leading to many visible incidents. Over the past 72-months key people owned facts that would have prevented harm and did not share the lifesaving details until after the carnage. This text will celebrate judgment; welcome our old friend as a lifesaving quality. Regardless of what we call it, the experience is a gift leading to correct predictions. When we respect and share the forecast resulting from our refined gift, we often avoid the storm.

Costa Concordia: A Predictable Loss

January 15, 2012, brought me and many others face to face with the Italian cruise disaster. She was a gorgeous ship two days earlier. Now, Lady Concordia was on the rocks, all but capsized after striking an underwater formation older and sturdier than all of us combined. The open wound in her hull resulted in at least 32 deaths, significant injuries, a handful of missing loved ones, and five fallen crew. Two of the missing victims were not found. This accident was preventable; no surprise to those in the industry of protection, accidents are always avoidable. The Costa Concordia Cruise was a significant example of small mistakes ending big and bad, positive intentions ending with tragic consequences, and unresolved conflicts leading to death.

The well-meaning captain had veered off-course intentionally, leaving safe passage to offer a "salute" from passengers on-board to the island residents of Giglio. Respecting old traditions in unfamiliar territory, a lesson I delve into later, urged the ship's captain to give passengers an enjoyable view beyond their expectations. He intended to make the once-in-a-lifetime cruise a dash better than the competing cruise-line. The accident undoubtedly led to a new experience for the passengers and crew, but it was nothing they had expected. It was just before 10 PM when part-two of the nightmare began. The massive boat, a floating vacation home for nearly 4300 women, children and men, 1023 considered crew, started to sink in the darkness.

Sound Judgment Fades

Costa Concordia, within the context of predictable and preventable harm, became the avatar of vulnerability as a human race. Mesmerized by her mass and elegance, humans were once again distracted by nature's dirty little trick. Fantasy, imagery, and unsinkable imagination are assets; however, the attributes of the ideal experience had ended ugly once again. Raising the bar, outdoing the competition, and pushing to be bigger and better for less money would be awfully expensive for the innocent passengers on the Costa Cruise. The Costa Concordia was suddenly destined to become the next tragic event. The common but deadly equation; absolute trust based on appearance, in a lion's den of predictable danger. Was this a case of negligence or recklessness? Was the crash an innocent mistake? Was it purely accidental, foreseen, or perhaps, as insurance carriers have said in the past, an act of God? Had the captain deviated from the norm, and does he have a reputation for risk-taking or Tombstone Courage, confusing bravery with reckless risk? Or was he doing what every cruise captain does in the blue Mediterranean Sea; leaving the busy traffic zone to offer an extraordinary experience?

Was it Predictable?

One fact, announced after the accident, swayed public opinion, including mine. A violation of tradition was about to suffer the wrath of global disdain. The captain committed a breach in protocol that would cast doubt on his judgment and post-accident response. His seemingly rational decision was fitting for a fearful passenger. It did not fit the expectations held for the position of a captain. His choice changed everything in the world-view and affected our generous ability to forgive. All but approximately 300 passengers and crew had left the ship, aligning with the instinctual drive to survive. Unlike many cases where the leader stayed with the boat, this was different. The captain left the ship before the full evacuation of the passengers; not a cause, but a glimpse into the mind. The former captain would end any chance of becoming a hero; instead, his judgment would leave him tagged a criminal and our newest villain.

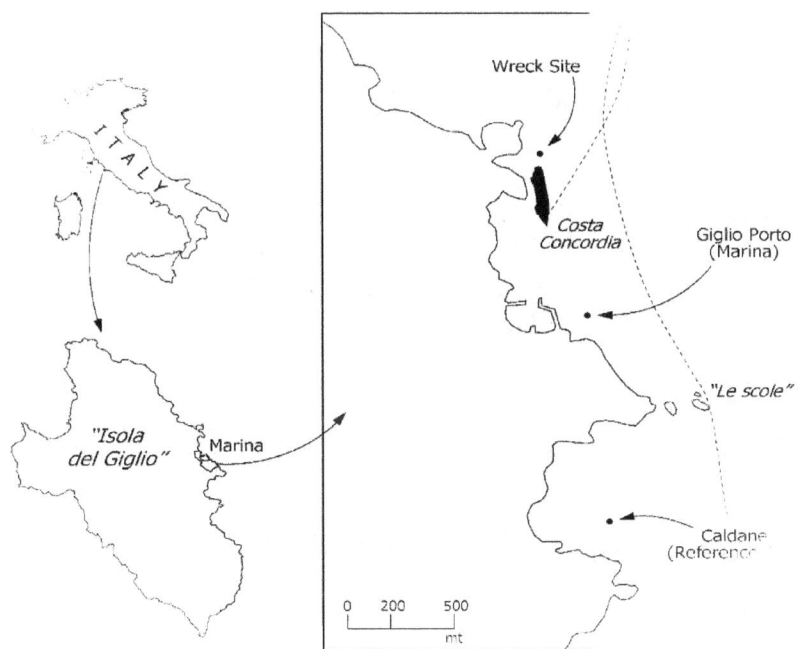

What was the Distraction?

The latest disaster, while horrid and raw, was another case of predictable harm, a dramatic example of a common mistake or calculated risk. A simple deviation from the norm, while tragic, led to a chain-of-events compounded by a flight from reality and failure to take responsibility. We are often a forgiving and gracious culture, willing to accept with open arms those who fail, and even unintentionally kill. As the Concordia captain learned in his rapid transition from executive leader to our greatest offender, mercy has a few rules of engagement. We appreciate those who fail, take responsibility, and share the lessons learned. In this case, we suspected a mistake had been made but were shocked when the captain side-stepped responsibility by stepping in front of those waiting in line for a lifeboat.

As the human condition demands in a crisis, old instincts kicked in for the captain; fear, stress, and emotion had increased, followed by a forceful reaction of diminished logic (figure 1). Reasonable rules had fled the scene, and a strange form of selfishness blew through the wheelhouse owning the soul of the captain. The heroism exercised by others over the past one thousand years didn't apply. Something had softened the backbone of a trusted man.

The courage needed or summoned from God or guts and supported in ancient scrolls of maritime tradition had been crowded out. His stress and a self-centered need for survival is not an excuse, but a teachable moment many have missed. Most will admit to smaller examples of reacting adversely under stress; however, we shouldn't acquiesce to the captain's rationale. A lengthy list of pilots and workers have responded in similar circumstances and respected the tradition. Custom had a purpose, not only for the captain, but the 4000 passengers relying on the captain to elevate their safety over his.

Overwhelm

Call it a policy, the tradition, or tag it a standard operating procedure, the rules went out the window on Lady Concordia, like other cases that never make the international news. Overwhelm and emotional distress decrease logic and reasoning; not an opinion but a law of performance science. When our distractions and stress lead to an unkind word or error it rarely makes the news. In this case, distress hit the global headlines after a major change in behavior. With every new threshold, stress often creates novel and disturbing human manners. Increased pressure is one of the most popular and useful predictors of injury and error. Training, self-awareness, and a commitment to continuous communication help reduce our exposure to harm. The Concordia captain only had two of the requirements moments before the fatal accident. His deviation from a pattern of sound judgment tells us he was likely experiencing an unusual internal or external distraction. Determine the disturbance, and you often expose another element of predictable harm, improving the atmosphere needed in a culture of safety. The risk of injury increases with any distraction, and the Concordia Wheelhouse was running with a list of disturbing possibilities. Passengers and the public would eventually learn the pain was inflicted by one of today's usual suspects. Safe communication, typically the mandatory tool in any wheelhouse, had become a conditional luxury.

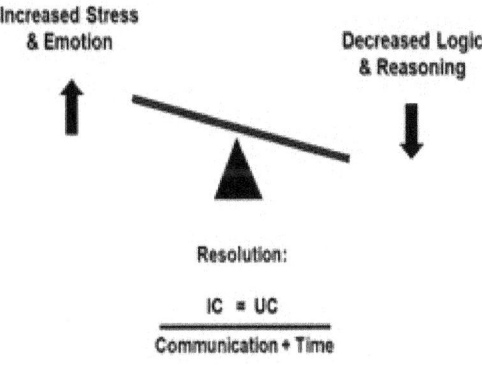

Figure 1: Describes the impacts of new stressors leading to the reduction of logic, reasoning, and short-term memory. The formula at the bottom of the graphic provides the solution, describing how understanding returns over time and is accelerated with consistent communication *(I see what you see, with communication, reasonably delivered over time).*

Normal Route, Abnormal Performance

The eight-year-old Costa Concordia had been on the first leg of a well-traveled route around the Mediterranean Sea with 4,229 passengers and crew on board. She deviated from her planned path at the Isola del Giglio, sailing closer than expected and hitting the rock formation on the sea floor. Some say the navigational mistake was an error of a few degrees on the standard compass. The sound was reportedly terrifying. The screech and groan of a ship mortally wounded by a 180-foot gash in the hull would not be the last scare. While some were unaware of the cause, all electrical power was lost, and seawater rushed into the lower portions of the dark ship. Absolute terror preceded death as over thirty innocent victims, some children, entered the water. For some, a wall of water met them. A few would float, some would sink at once, and others suffered a horrifying final breath taken from the last small gap near the ceiling of their private cabin. In the end, 64 passengers were injured and 32 died, all interrupted while eating, dancing, playing on the deck and sleeping.

"Do What You Know You Should Be Doing:"

Reactions climaxed during the six-hour rescue effort as a Search and Rescue Commander traveling to the scene realized he was talking to the ship's captain. The words "Where are you?" crackled through the lines of marine and mobile communications, part of recorded messages I reviewed lasting eight hours. "I am on a rescue boat near the ship" explained Captain Francesco Schettino. The rescue commander followed up, asking, "What rescue effort can you coordinate from there? Go back to the ship."

Captain Schettino's response came after a long delay, far too long considering he is seated as a passenger on a rescue craft. He need only answer a question the Galley Busboy could have answered at once. Finally, the captain responded, "I am in a boat near the Concordia. "The rescue commander exploded with adrenaline-fueled anger and disbelief as the reality hit him. His outrage, he would later explain, included a captain completing his shift in safety as drowning victims, and those threatened by severe injury only hope to survive. The rescue commander responded with a vastly different tone, cadence, and volume. "I order you to get back on the ship," he screamed, "Find a rope ladder near the bodies in the water, climb back on board and coordinate the rescue. Do what you know you should be doing. You don't need to go to the comfort of your home."

It was true, Captain Schettino knew what to do in an emergency at sea yet breached his duty-owed the passengers and crew. I quickly marked the transcript with a note in the margin, *why was he distracted?* This case qualified for the text. No Further Harm, a philosophy and higher standard, respects mistakes, but rarely tolerates the second-sin. Harm should never increase after the first tragedy, and we must drill down on the details of all errors after the event as well. Something was horribly wrong with the post-accident rescue, and it seemed to start in the wheelhouse abandoned by Schettino. While most passengers made it safely to shore and called relatives, Captain Schettino made it to land and was taken directly to jail. Why? Accidents happen, humans make mistakes, and leadership is not a perfect science. Why would blame reach the captain and avoid Costa Crociere International, the company?

The investigation focused on shortcomings in the procedures followed by the captain, an easy mark considering all possibilities. I later found most everyone on-board rescue vessels, co-masters leaving the ship's bridge, and those listening knew something was wrong. Beyond the collision, the captain's behavior was a deviation from the norm, something repeated in too many cases and throughout this book. But why he deviated from his training, a complete scenario, would be delayed for years. The entire plot eventually made sense and found its way into this book.

The Threat is Contained, Let's Move On!

Former Captain Schettino was found guilty of manslaughter and sentenced to sixteen years in prison, approximately six months for each life lost. Then, only after all testimony had been provided, would I get the unique opportunity to interact with two sources close to the investigation. The purpose of the meeting was to extract lessons, teachable material, and the predictable elements of the Costa Concordia incident. Unfortunately, those armed with lifesaving information were not ready to share. They summed up the whole scenario with one statement: *"Maritime safety includes a few universal laws; when the Master of the ship breaks the rules, the whole ship is unsafe. We believe all fruit becomes tainted by the poisonous tree."*

The beautiful words, while scripted and flawlessly delivered, left me frustrated. Had I burned valuable time and money for a sweet quote instead of a solution? I spoke with a handful of others changed by the event. In the end, the short meeting with the maritime officials-became-philosophers had value. The lesson would become a golden thread that weaves its way through most humanmade tragedies. Secrecy or a flawed definition of confidentiality is a contributor to harm, which begs for a solution.

Findings & Unnecessary Delay

Italian leaders remained tightlipped, even after advancing questions and my motive. The trial was over, the former captain is in jail, and the ship is slated for salvage. Why all the caution and secrecy? Many of my questions remained unanswered: Is the lesson found in the safety-persona of the captain? Does culpability reach beyond the captain? Did he deviate from the regular route? Is it past-practice? Has he been involved in similar incidents?

I would soon be schooled in longstanding tradition, and a popular barrier to safety. *Those fully qualified to supply life-saving details after an incident, often go silent.* Seemingly small and embarrassing details become secrets as they had in the Concordia Wheelhouse that night. Italian officials shifted all their energy to the one who allegedly poisoned the tree. Captain Schettino faced trial and was sentenced to prison. The reliable information applicable to predictable and preventable harm was virtually locked up that night. Eventually, I asked if their speech was restricted due to legal advice. No. If not a legal matter, it must be cultural.

Like my professional peers and others, I'm no longer

comfortable with incomplete stories or the logic behind the aloof rationale for harm. I have no problem with the incarceration of the captain but locking up the information we desperately need is a second-sin we should reject. There lies the cultural challenge; tragic, high-value, corporate-level events often end without proper and prompt life-saving solutions shared by those with the information.

Cautions, equipment issues, and flaws found in the avoidance of crucial conversations make the shortlist of life-saving data postponed. Delay due to legal and investigative needs contributes to the deadly gap; not a moment but a long, long postponement of vital data. We might legally shuffle around the truth but cannot defend this type of delay any longer. We must try to supply tentative answers to crucial questions on the minds of peer industries, leaders, parents and safety officers throughout the region. If we genuinely believe in preventing further harm as soon as possible, these questions need prompt, even partial answers:

1. Was it predictable?
2. What was the distraction?
3. Does it call for conversation, intervention or penalty?
4. Is the cause trending?
5. What is the teachable resolution or short-term fix?

Officials argue the information and Concordia's after-action report was availed to all who asked. Right, in-part, we did access a final report after waiting for nearly two years. Even after the severe delay, contents were often lofty, academic, and sanitized, making the sluggish findings virtually useless in future prevention. The report shared how the ship sank, rather than why. The full color document was gorgeous, highlighting the speed of incoming seawater and angle-of-submersion. Compass readings, how seawater cutoff power, and how backup systems failed rounded a sterile report, which looked more like ad copy promoting a cruise. The investigative report was packed with technical data, compliance language, and old training records. I've reviewed or conducted thousands of criminal and safety investigations; the Concordia report looked familiar for all the wrong reasons. Authors get five-stars for the technical aspect, but the report failed the real-world sniff test.

Thanks for What, We Need to Know Why

I read every word, the complete report, and repeated the task. I examined reactions to the document. Our culture willingly accepts the average investigation telling us **what** happened when we need to know **why**. Two essential elements about conditions at sea were missing from the 181-plus pages. The lesson would remain woefully incomplete until we understood the head and the heart of Captain Francesco Schettino. The case study was suspended as incomplete.

The fatal Concordia accident was seemingly another tragedy with unanswered questions. Once again, the report read like an academic mystery, avoiding the inevitable; the chief cause in most crashes and intentional acts. Human Factors caused the sinking of Costa Concordia, and human factors are difficult to determine or fully understand. Because the elusive cause is tough to discern and discuss, we often exclude the major contributor from our findings after a tragedy. The actual conditions, the heart of leadership and the human formulas fueling the gut-level decisions, are missing from many investigative reports. These are vital details we can no longer deny, creating real and measurable hazards.

In the case of Concordia, information qualifying as *Human Factors* was known, but not shared as a future point of prevention. The necessary and prompt conversation seemed to stop with the arrest of Francesco Schettino. The final report was published nearly two years later, literally enough time to build a new cruise ship. The report did not address tangible solutions. Investigators insisted they were fact-finders, deferring any human performance solutions to the cruise ship operator and the employer. I braced for the predictable corporate response, and it came. Costa Crociere told the world they would rely on the fact-finders, deferring to investigators for recommendations. The truth faded in the familiar space between those investigating tragedy and those responsible.

One of the omissions included the contagion of flawed leadership, and how members on the bridge likely caught the same strain Schettino was spreading. Performance science has verified the attitude of the top leader is contagious. Poor communication supported by a disconnectedness with his chain of subordinates was a reality. The full power of the toxic strain would later become clear by the arrest and criminal charges levied against those closest to Schettino, further supporting suspicions about conduct in the bridge prior to impact.

Distraction and Silence Killed Lady Concordia

The Costa Concordia accident was the result of simple human flaws. A petty conflict, garnished with ego and pride, was compounded by an ever-popular distraction. Without intervention, the flaw, fed by conceit, continued to morph into the popular silent-treatment causing 64 serious injuries and 32 deaths. An immature communication breakdown, and tuning-out members of the team, added to the eerie, child-like silence between two key leaders leading to the sinking of Costa Concordia. Because the leader continuously avoided seemingly petty problems, tragedy was predictable and inevitable. Human factors in the form of conflict-communication breakdowns rarely make the final report. In the case of Lady Concordia, the 181-page investigative findings dance around an issue we find in far too many cases. The Costa Concordia sunk because two leaders were angry and stopped sharing information necessary to pilot the ship. Mid-managers and others seeing the immature behavior and equally distracted, didn't have the courage and permission to intervene.

Prompt Data Saves Lives

Investigators, attorneys, and corporate representatives often insist on having the proof before they share, rather than enough data to save a life. In tragedies, this often translates to having enough time to delay an unfortunate and embarrassing detail. Humans need cause-information when our concerns are fresh even when that information is uncomfortable to share. This fatal delay and softening of robust advice are cultural flaws on a global scale. In the case of Concordia, other ship captains needed immediate information related to the seaworthiness of vessels. They were left begging for data that might lead to the prevention of a similar tragedy. Their requests were likely unanswered, and they went ahead with rumors and sketchy information about the loss of Costa Concordia.

U.S. Maritime investigators needed data, port officials and cruise ship mechanics had an immediate need for clarification. Most pressing, relatives had an urgent need for information. The curious and perceived slight eventually led to a financial hit, which included thousands of potential cruise passengers who needed to know what had happened. Left in the dark and with little information, potential passengers drew their conclusions, and without proper data withdrew their plans. Excluding cruise ship travel in the near and distant future, vacationers invested discretionary dollars on a safer experience.

NOTE: Concordia's Support Team and First-Responders were praised for their sensitive treatment of relatives and survivors.

Learning from Cultural Flaws

In addition to cancellations or reversals of cruise reservations, the flawed, incomplete, and delayed access to facts also led to a call for expensive inspections of seaworthy vessels. Inspectors across the globe were pressured to conduct risky and unnecessary work. Uncertain of the evidence, possibilities rather than facts haunted workers. An estimated two-billion-dollar shipping accident affected stakeholders; estimates due to the disaster response and passenger abandonment may exceed an added one billion dollars. The added cost of collateral activities beyond the Concordia collision, which include the death of a salvage professional, currently exceeds $700 million. The lifesaving benefits and ethical considerations of timeliness and shared data are supported by history. Unnecessary delays or refusing to share known findings by Costa Concordia are only one example supporting a negative and universal pattern calling for a cultural shift.

Early Assumptions Equal Incomplete Conclusions

The Concordia story highlights how any safety or criminal investigation fixed on a solo-cause typically ends with a solo-cure. This case includes the egregious behavior of a maritime offender; however, the unacceptable performance goes beyond Captain Francesco Schettino. As my professional brothers and sisters in the industry of protection already know, we risk falling into a trap after a massive crisis or a controversial injury. When the investigation reveals a significant mistake by a key employee, we often delay sharing. When findings may be embarrassing, we continually reconsider the data. In some cases, we disguise our lack-of-candor as a brilliant legal strategy. When weighing a decision between showing prompt safety tips and the exposure to civil lawsuits, corporate culture may slow-walk lifesaving disclosures over risking a financial hit. Not just my opinion, but a fact pattern (outlined in chapter two). Corporate culture, and many public sector leaders, credited for high-value and historical successes, also commits the occasional atrocity found in silence when information may save a life.

"Silence has become an organizational phenomenon, expressions of serious opinion, important ideas, and sharing safety concerns are dying for many reasons. Fear of opposition and general disagreement top the list."

– Dr. Said Rezabeygi, Azad University, East Azerbaijan. February 6, 2019.

Far too often we punish the one who allegedly poisoned the tree but do not address the culture that tainted the taproot long before the incident. It is unconventional and borderline offensive to dig deeper into the *why*. We stop short of the whole lesson, I certainly have. I hope to drop the practice as the silence is a moral infraction at times, and criminal in the case of Lady Concordia.

Hurt Employees Hurt Operations

Like many others, I would rather avoid the tough questions about contributing factors; weighing the causative influences equals a complex investigation. The rare dive below the surface feels more like a visit to the Mariana Trench. The disclosure offers a compelling experience when you reveal the broader issues, specifically, for the first-time. It's never a short or straightforward conversation when we explore the human factors, such as the role of fatigue, preoccupation, insomnia, a hangover, new medication or quitting a drug. We may see the need to go deeper to prevent predictable harm, but we avoid the painful journey of examining layers of culture, attitudes, risky behaviors off the clock, and those unchallenged traditions and outdated policies on the clock. By finding and relying on the solo-cause such as Captain Schettino, we incrementally drift away from the so-called soft-stuff affecting safety and care.

Avoiding the complex, life-saving exercise is the preference of most; dodging the fact that a key person was absent at the time of the accident, refraining from tough questions to determine disputes were out of control with the whole crew. Solo cause theory might miss evidence of the overburdened peer; a mid-shipman in a dual or three-headed role, doing more than one person should do. Our old thinking and traditions may minimize realities of exhaustion and anger. The single cause and sole blame often dodge the loss of trust and loyalty on a ship. A human factor called apathy was also present, ending with reckless behavior. Hardest of the soft stuff on Concordia included the clear erosion of morale, known to increase mistakes and injuries.

The Costa Concordia incident includes an extensive list of these potentially impactful secondary conditions. The Hollywood mentality found in many official inquiries prefers a villain; visible harm and tragedy need a host. When we're not careful we create the host in people like Captain Francesco Schettino. He has been tagged an irresponsible carrier in the eyes of the global safety community; our icon of disgust, potentially ending our lesson prematurely. I'm disgusted with the captain as well; however, we're searching for solutions over another public flogging. Rapid investigations are the norm; too little examination, rushed conclusions, and compliance-based findings leading to missed lessons. Each lesson missed returns as another casualty. I'm compelled to repeat the reality in training; **each lesson missed after an accident or act returns as another casualty.** This is not an opinion, but a fact-pattern found in performance science. Safety lessons have a fixed, nonnegotiable price. We pay now or we pay later; delay or choose to pay.

The quality of the Concordia investigation is debatable; however, the containment was swift and visible as officials considered Francesco contained and no longer a threat within hours of the crisis. The outrage of the coast guard, the top news story billing, the global disgust after the tragic accident, and the lengthy prison sentence camouflaged the actual cause, which we almost missed entirely.

Again, I'm not absolving the captain of responsibility. I'm merely enlarging the footprint of contributing factors, and it calls for added scrutiny and painful lessons. When we focus on a solo cause, we find it, and often bypass a lifesaving education and correctable flaws. We miss the secondary causes, major contributors in the case of Lady Concordia. There lies the difference between traditional safety programs and the spirit of No Further Harm, which expands the solution over the blame.

A Complete Investigation Always Includes Human Factors

Investigations are never complete until we examine the so-called soft-stuff; clues and cues available prior to the incident, accident, and the intentional act. Predictable Harm changes how we evaluate each casualty, big or small, and we do it in our analysis of past events and disasters. No Further Harm also defends a quiet and confidential examination of the victim. Unresolved conflicts and distractions are considered soft-skills, placing them in the low-priority menu for change. Unfortunately, soft-stuff is quickly becoming the primary cause of loss and casualties. Minimizing the soft-skills has fatal consequences. Compelling evidence will be provided throughout the book, asking you to make the final call. The spirit of No Further Harm includes a healthy attitude and calls for more contemplation; moving the camera back, we become more preventative, while accepting the occasional need for the penalty. Plus, the proposed shift in thinking, the philosophy of No Further Harm, asks you to consider safety solutions as a mission rather than another safety or corporate policy. Lifesaving details, a human right, should never be concealed or delayed due to selfish concerns. Sharing the minimum may be acceptable in matters of discipline, but it is no longer acceptable when additional lives are threatened.

Key Factors Sinking Lady Concordia

Leaders on the bridge had missed the predictable clues, the so-called soft stuff or human factors leading to disastrous outcomes. *Avoidance or fear had killed communications*, producing a dark, morale-busting tone in the wheelhouse. In addition to the captain's errors, reliable sources say the command bridge was the scene of other *unlawful distractions*. Not a surprise, but a sign of the times as *mobile phone use* was standard. Some *tuned-out the noise with earbuds and personal music on personal devices*. *Unauthorized guests* toured the bridge, adding to an extensive list of minor things leading to a major loss. None of the small vices are problematic in the comfort of a private cabin; however, prohibited in the wheelhouse by Maritime Law and Concordia Policy.

The most egregious, arguably predictable distraction and performance flaw is found in the Control Room of the Helmsman. The Helm, who controls the rudder steering the ship, allegedly *"Misheard" the emergency order* to hard-turn the rudder. He reportedly *slammed the rudder in the wrong direction*, ending any chance of avoiding the rocks below. Italian was not his primary language, but he embraced the universal language offered on PlayStation. The language barrier, and the Helmsman's obsessive attachment to PlayStation, were announced for the first-time during the trial. While I believe the language barrier trivial, I suspect the lure of video games weighed-in as a contributing factor. Neither language nor electronic games were given legal weight in judicial findings. Mobile-pings tell us ship leaders likely ended their portable obsessions when the collision was inevitable, and moments before the ear-piercing screech of fatal injury to the hull. Like driving, texting, and finding yourself in the oncoming lane, dropping the distraction once the collision is inevitable has no affect. Your fate is sealed, like those who caused the sinking of Lady Concordia.

Review: Five Recommended Questions

No Further Harm asks us to *Respect* five considerations in the prevention of acts or accidents, and *Respond* following advice found in twelve core concepts outlined in chapter six. I encourage the unconventional *Review* of incidents and accidents by answering five helpful questions. This healthy triage may unearth details. The simple recommendation is considered a minimum after any crisis, big or small:

1. Was it predictable? Yes, the fatal Costa Concordia accident was avoidable and predictable. Once we find the elements of predictability, all factors including each human factor, the sketch leads to improvements and remedial or new training to consider. Every rule violation in the wheelhouse of Concordia was another clue of foreseeable harm. Concordia also lacked the checks and balances of leadership. Like a problem the airline industry has corrected, the command structure must include a process to question the commander. Airlines have shifted to CRM (Cockpit Resource Management), which set policy for calling out the boss when air operations get dangerous. Before CRM, co-pilots risked a lawful silence when words were needed. I know of no such policy on Italian-based cruise ships, who seem entrenched in old traditions of Command and Control in both private and public policy.

2. What was the distraction? The preoccupation of the ship's captain includes workload, fatigue, conflicts, mobile devices, people-pleasing, past-practice, and possibly a dose of apathy. All elements of predictable harm, I would place these on the training and discussion list of priorities. Distractions are usually innocent oversights and include administrative apathy, and other factors that de-emphasize safety. A distraction includes anything, internal or external, with enough force to disrupt focus. A diversion may consist of temporary illness, injury, or a pending layoff. It may include a nasty argument with a loved one, a twisted ankle, or a child in trouble at school. In the final analysis, any distraction may lead to harm. The ship's captain had an extensive list of potential distractions; professional and personal problems were interfering with his judgment.

3. Does it call for conversation, intervention or penalty? The Costa Concordia incident includes a violation of existing rules, laws, and lasting traditions. It is normal to consider new regulations after every tragedy, the expensive and often unnecessary implementation based on the innate desire to prevent a repeat performance. Many respected professionals jump into a flawed intervention based on guilt, producing new legislation, penalties, and policy on the heels of the crisis. We need not pour money into a new solution when recurring problems only call for more attention on existing guidelines. While the penalty is in-play with the incarceration of the ship's captain, the conversation has and will continue to amend human behavior over other alternatives. In my experience, and with few exceptions, everything from the prevention of minor accidents to mass shootings fall within existing rules and an emphasis on clear and continuous communication.

4. Is the cause trending? The loss of a famous cruise ship is not the 'trend' we look for in applying the leverage outlined in No Further Harm. Underlying problems and cyclic conditions are the trends we hope to expose. Once found, shared awareness lowers risk at once. In the Concordia case, we find a cycle of apathy, fatigue, increased workloads, absolute distractions, and symptoms ignored. Even with the multi-tasking myth debunked, safety remained compromised. The Concordia is another example of too much activity in a small and dangerous workspace. The flaw is most popular when loyal people are afraid to call out the trend. This form of compromised safety isn't limited to the Concordia; certain sectors continue to overload individuals and the environment, even with symptoms increasing. Simple mistakes, minor injuries, and a rise in interpersonal conflicts often trend before the crisis strikes. When we catch the small signs and trends, politely share the obvious, we usually avoid the disaster.

5. What is the teachable resolution or short-term fix? The short-term fix includes existing guidelines. Avoiding a seemingly natural over-reaction, the Concordia calls for affirmation of current laws, traditions, and well-established Maritime Regulation. Enforcement and correction are underway, the result of existing standards. The short-term fix was available before the cruise ship crisis. The lesson is attention to detail and the courage to engage in continuous communication; assets lost or nonexistent on the Concordia.

Chapter Conclusion:

There exists a beneficial tool in evaluating our individual and collective safety; vulnerable and risky targets, including those previously injured, have the template we need. Our prevention tools are within the mind and past behavior of both victim and cause. The profile of our risk is readily available, and this form of research makes the solution more accessible. Found by those with the courage to discuss the predictable path, we learn through the eyes of those who drifted off the trail. Those who have suffered as the injured or with the wounded; those dropped to their knees due to unfortunate harm and habits hold the long-term solution. The cultural barrier includes yesterday's victims who own the knowledge we need for today's safety. We often avoid the victim, considering their input protected or off-limits.

QuikTip:

"Suggest alternatives. Never assume a 'better way' has been considered."

The risk found on the bridge of Costa Concordia is ever-present in all environments; searching for a host while silently drifting thru homes, job sites, airports, highways, famous nightclubs, elementary schools, and any location where humans congregate. We make the mistake of passively waiting for risk to knock on our front door while he's already seated comfortably in our favorite chair. We tend to wait for the attack close to home or postpone action and conversation, waiting for good intelligence and information. As the text illustrates, we have the needed knowledge, information, and a portrait for our current adversary, which is the risk we do not recognize, discuss, and respect. The time may have come to shift the debate away from a clinical or academic argument about predictable harm.

This book avoids the academic interpretation of risk. It is not a thesis about the defensible risk instruments or a predictive algorithm. The text highlights how to recognize danger and avoid the tragic outcome. The book will not bore you with controlled trials of violence, properties of clinical intervention, or how diet may negatively affect your safety. This book has time-tested, victim approved, rapid solutions producing lower risk via greater awareness. We will remove seemingly reasonable excuses for poor planning or for not having a plan-in-play. Survival is an attitude, rarely a case of luck. Like morale, safety is a spirit, and a gut-level commitment. Policy means little if we do not spread the sense gleaned from recent events. Safety is a core value, which means nothing without leadership, even if that includes going down with the ship.

End of Chapter One

NOTES

CHAPTER TWO

Safety: A Changing Culture

The realities of injury and loss rarely qualify as a light topic; the in-depth review of innocent accidents, job site safety, the active-shooter, and the victim-profile usually involve a serious discussion. Outside the industry of protection, the awkward subject matter can stall a conversation or prove counterproductive. I hope to change the stigma with my friends and clients, making every accident, unexpected blow-up, assault, and catastrophic event a training opportunity.

Chapter two addresses safety culture; capturing lessons as each occurrence unfolds, leading to constant improvement. While a premature chat on the heels of disaster seems clunky and abhorrent, prompt communication pays big. I hope to make an impression with the reader that with your help and a few course corrections this seemingly tricky cultural shift is doable. No Further Harm is within reach for those committed to a conversation rather than a battle. The prevention of intentional or accidental injury to loved ones, employees, and our community-family begs for more than light contemplation or frothy political stance.

Reframing our Relationship with Harm

Harm is too harsh to avoid, too complicated to gloss over, and a discussion far too critical to exclude. While this project involves more than a book and intends to meet several aims, replacing fear-based avoidance with useful information and deliberate change are the primary drivers. This book is part of a strategy in-play, a plan that appears to work. By increasing the conversation around forecasting and creating a culture recognizing predictable harm, we're decreasing unreasonable fear and lowering risk. I'm inviting you to give it a try.

Reframing our relationship with injury and loss has become a matter of influence and leadership. This quick chapter will introduce a proposed shift in thinking. Depending on your role and relationship to the topic, the motivation will hopefully lead to long-term interest and conversation beyond the book. The goal calls for a little information, backbone, and the guts to say we can do much better than we have in the recent past. The missing elements and the proposition of this text include four specific areas:

1. While predicting harm is a preventative action, it calls for the detailed examination of past acts, incidents, and accidents. How we evaluate recent casualties, specifically victims, affect the future of safety.

2. Evidence shows we are suffering from competing values. The rapid communication necessary for preventing harm is in collision with hypersensitivity and the fear of offending others.

3. Our intuitive sense to recognize a threat has been compromised by distractions. The full-time flow of data and related interruptions is now a key contributor to serious injury and premature death. Irrefutable evidence will support the theory.

4. Visible accidents and humanmade tragedies are often blamed erroneously on process and equipment. With natural disasters being the only exception, Human factors have

stepped up as a formidable threat to safety.

The ideal culture of safety calls on a workgroup, family, or the individual willing to forecast risk; habitually reconsidering and redefining the environment. No Further Harm will be defined in detail and through facts; buffered with opinion and empowering you to judge your surroundings and draw your conclusions. We will share tools and techniques applied by safety experts, private sector practitioners, and include other straightforward applications. I'll emphasize the newest assessment model; a 5-stage hybrid and method. The application is finding success, shared publicly for the first time through this publication.

"Where all think alike, no one thinks very much."

- Walter Lippmann

When it comes to the policy and politics of intentional harm and personal protection, the debating society has several meaningful goals; however, a prompt resolution doesn't appear to be one of them. Individual risk and liability are wildly different than most could ever dream. Storming at various times, elevations, and with a range of variance, many do not understand elevated risk. This book explains the realities of life-long dangers while promoting a strategy for the moment. We will venture into history with the sole purpose of improving individual safety in the present day.

Our goal includes influencing safe decisions in the next 24 to 72 hours; well-deserved and necessary for the peaceful enjoyment of family, colleagues, and friends, with or without being armed. We will plan our project or day but postpone lofty Quarterly Reports and Five-Year Strategic Plans. Long-term planning has a purpose, but true safety is within the fence-line of today. Preventable harm is best-served day-by-day and in the present. Our concern about accidents and intentional harm can be consuming; however, quality of life improves for those who understand risk. When safety becomes a priority, our personal and professional relationships, marketing, profitability, and wellness improve. As Abraham Maslow has shared, a perception of safety shepherds the journey toward personal and professional success. Everything worthwhile relies first on a sense of security and a belief that we are safe. What's missing from Maslow's message is our direct responsibility and obligation to others.

When Thoughts Change, Environments Change

I believe a profound change will be necessary to meet personal and professional safety priorities on the horizon. Responsibility had already made the shift from a reliance on rigid rules. Regulatory bibles related to work injuries and applying to every human condition are not popular. We only absorb a small amount of valuable information from the black and white rules, the intellectual side of safety education. More policy hasn't worked, and Active Shooter Training Skills offered a band aid. The less-than-empowering response of Run, Hide, Attack, is not the answer I was hoping for. The lack of solutions tells me we are ready for a cultural change. When our advisors at the federal level suggest how we should zig and zag under active gunfire, and which janitorial closet offers the best hiding place, we are ready for a cultural change.

It would appear the future is up to you and me, sentenced to a life of complaining or committing to a safety makeover. Gut-level influence, not the academic formula, continues to save lives. In my opinion, we have a few options left. On or off the job, safety is a matter of the head and the heart. When you combine both, you are on your way to fresh thoughts and a safer environment. Continuous communication and a closer examination of the victim-experience have what we need. Beyond the losses and wins, the raw reality may soon dominate center stage. After a record-breaking year, and thanks to the Active-Shooter, a shift is inevitable and may be more effective. The rules of safety will always be needed; however, empowering people with the skills to predict harm and criminal victimization take it to a new level. Mentors, employees, parents and teachers armed with heart-level motivation and full-spectrum forecasting skills will make up the core movement.

Once the side-by-side examination is complete, rigid rules versus forecasting skills, there should be no doubt. Academic and intellectual standards are important, but no longer most important. Our formulas, reports, and spreadsheets are a must, but gut-level courage is the missing element. Those who influence culture with the stories, skills, and examples are quickly becoming the key players. Those who support existing safety formulas with clear illustrations, a dash of care, the local reality, and include the victim experience are more potent leaders. Only a small handful of those within our reach prefer another set of black and white rules.

Attitudes & Beliefs

I often ask myself and colleagues, what are the golden nuggets contributing to personal safety? What obligation do I have to contribute to a positive safety culture? What should my neighbors expect from me? Do you believe in No Further Harm? Should our schools be locked down due to fear? Do you protect others out of respect? Do you question dangerous procedures or leave it for someone else? Is it all about policy and law or are you dedicated to the best outcome for your team and family? Do you do the right thing based on the Excel spreadsheet of injury costs or due to the care for others? Heart-level influence, the obligation to protect, is occasionally missing from our safety message, a philosophy supporting a secure future. The necessary shift appears to include more than merely noticing danger. Our culture is begging for leaders willing to share and explain risk; tactfully educating others in the process, and holding others responsible for looking, listening, and sharing the subtle hints of danger. Because you continue to read this text, I believe you are one of the powerful resources willing to lead cultural change.

Forecasting: Harnessing Existing Fears

The heat of responsibility is increasing for both the private sector and local government. Some have asked for it, some beg for it, and others are terrified by the notion of shared-skills around protection. Then it happened, 2017 ushered in a series of incidents and accidents. Life-changing stuff to children and others forcing us to take a stand, return to the old arguments, or do it differently.

I've experienced the angst of a cultural clash several times during my life. Knowledge and skills become available, the tools could greatly reduce harm, but some believe educated men and women would abuse what is meant to empower. Forecasting is one of those skills. Not only forecasting violence but predicting and preventing injuries on and off the clock. Forecasting is a life sustaining skill-set. Individual safety professionals are starting to feel it. Our job in leadership is no longer about ensuring adults feel safe. Leadership is tasked with something more daunting. We must convince others to create a culture of safety; take responsibility for specific skills and training, to predict and prevent harm

is the calling. Avoiding extremes is crucial; sidestepping paranoia and shunning bulletproof machismo allow the transition.

The safety renovation era and the development of individual skills are upon us; predicting and preventing accidents, injury, and assault is on the way to becoming a popular upgrade. Much like learning a martial art, a new language, or improving the skills needed to sketch or paint a portrait, the culture of safety and developing the art of forecasting takes practice. This text offers the basics needed to launch, improve, and hone the ability to forecast and redirect the energy wasted on risky habits.

We can reform our thoughts, words, and actions supporting a more predictable journey and for the most part, the ideal environment recognizing foreseeable harm. Individuals that understand the art and science of forecasting risk, have less stress, little confusion about their observations, and they are more likely to remain fearless and highly productive for all the right reasons.

Popular Culture

In my experience, every human can claim feeling and intuition as innate; a skill or gift at birth, which some deny or mistrust. Most counterproductive to a gut-level guidance system is the unconditional surrender to the punishing popular culture demanding we drop all judgment due to the risk of bias. This text advocates improving how we judge rather than a risky removal of human belief. Predicting harm and recognizing danger is our goal; qualifying why and how present conditions increase the need for refined and rapid analysis. Bias will occur as we forecast our surroundings, and that is no reason to throw out this beautiful baby with the bath water.

QuikTip:

"Don't minimize a threat out of false respect or misguided tolerance."

Biased observations are part of the human thought process, and every choice we make includes personal preference and individual history. A culture supporting No Further Harm does not condone or promote any biased behavior or other "isms." Under this change, we recognize bias, make the course-correction, and stay on the path.

This important journey includes judging the human risks before us.

Under the umbrella of No Further Harm, we treat biased opinions in predicting harm with the same corrective energy applied to other missteps; we listen, discuss it, and measure the error. Was it a matter of innocence, ignorance or malice? Anything more extreme than a simple correction will paralyze the change-process needed for predicting harm and preventing violence. Most understand the paralysis resulting from overcorrecting an honest error; the results of punishing innocent mistakes. My research found peers, employers, and activists often criticize those who dare to judge risk. Those interviewed described being uninvited to meetings, told to reduce all warning and safety concerns to a constipated and written process, and a few were fired. Some of the same employers were later found celebrating the silence as success or diversity. Optimum safety is propped up by first-rate communication, and that calls for middle-ground, minus hypersensitive reactions.

A significant challenge to the safety is today's fear related to what others may think or do. We worry that our expression of concern is wrong. We stop to ponder the possible damage in cautioning others over the consequences of silence in the face of certain  danger. We wonder if we'll face persecution as fundamentalists, moral-police or as disruptive employees and neighbors. Far too often, we are frightened by the discussion; warning others is measured carefully, and we hesitate to share observations. We stop short of expressing suspicions about our surroundings and the behavior of others. Many have done the research, and we can defend the cultural reality in retrospect; cases of preventable injury and predictable violence include those acts and accidents we could have stopped.

No Further Harm: A Purely Predictable Path

Good people have remained silent due to fear, confused by office politics, and some wary of smearing their image. When a flawed pattern involves good people consistently doing dangerous things, the problem is usually cultural rather than legal. As rough as it may sound, some are willing, albeit unaware, to die or watch others die, due to the fear of being shunned, flogged by social media, or selfish concerns about reputation.

Cultural Problem, Hiding Behind Legal Excuses

Contributors to this project have told me of their regretful failure to speak up before the tragedy. The FBI has arrived at the same conclusion. School shootings, faulty airline equipment, rage-based offenders, and impaired equipment operators allowed to continue working after the threat was known. It ended ugly. The guilt is devastating. All unnecessary pain, once we acknowledge our challenge is not legal, it is cultural. Legal concerns are often the battle cry of those missing the grave state of affairs in a breaking cultural crisis. The legal barrier is often an obstruction by those needing a coffee conversation over another courtroom battle. The cultural crisis and change are worth every cup, meeting, and conversation. Once explained, opponents soften and middle-ground is possible. No Further Harm needs little leverage beyond a broad discussion around documented facts.

Cultural Red Flags

Conflicts, missteps, and the temptation to cloak safety errors in a blanket of secrecy are not new. We find similar behaviors and painful results in every region of the globe and within multiple industries. Hiding the embarrassing conflict within Costa Concordia's Pilot Team was unnecessary. The mistake included details redacted and all-but-sealed when they were likely public information. Awkward is not one of the exceptions to public disclosure, and not worth hiding for over two years. The good news tells us personal and professional safety-success is still possible when we recognize the challenge as cultural rather than legal. Cultural change needs contemplation while respecting urgency and ending with clear communication; valuable but diminishing resources in the USA and beyond. Tight schedules, profit, and the reckless handling of lifesaving data elevate risk. I'm not advocating we drop our Kimono for all to see but recognize the erosion of ethics and communication about known hazards. The shift needs a healthy look in the rearview mirror; historical icons may help form the necessary proof and the cultural pattern.

Iconic Moments & Missed Opportunities

Avoiding, minimizing, or hiding a known threat until it leads to a single or mass casualty isn't new. But it is becoming more popular, and the motive is not merely profit-driven. The motive and host has shifted over a 40+-year timeline.

The Airline Industry has been forced to face the truth several times, in one case, hiding an existing mechanical flaw in active airliners. The Jackscrew, a part controlling the horizontal tail, was blamed for a crash off the Los Angeles coast, killing all 88 people on board. The Jackscrew defect was not new, and those in the airline industry did not inform passengers as they tried to quietly correct the deficiency without interrupting service.

The Federal Aviation Administration took a hit as well, unintentionally contributing to Jackscrew infamy by acquiescing in the airline's decision to stretch out maintenance intervals. It would prove to be a fatal deviation from the norm in established practices. The National Transportation Safety Board (NTSB), responsible for investigations affecting transportation and US interests, cited "widespread systemic deficiencies." AKA: A policy or established practice leading to a pattern of unnecessary risks, accidents, and fatalities. The flaw and related design, before the 88 deaths, needed rapid decisions and clear communication; however, decisions slowly came to a full-stop and discussion decreased before the pivotal tragedy.

The Automobile Industry was dangerously quiet about an exploding gas tank, and curiously silent when a vehicle manufacturing flaw often slapped the vehicle into a fatal 180-degree spin. They would delay warnings again when airbags killed children and suffer self-imposed silence once more when the airbag lacerated the throat of the driver it was supposed to protect.

The Retail and Pharmaceutical Industry delayed warnings when cyanide poison was added to medicine, leading to multiple fatalities in a criminal case of product tampering. They continue to point fingers at others, interpreted as silence in relation to over 800 potentially dangerous supplements sold over-the-counter.

Food Service hampered efforts to announce e-coli (feces) in our hamburger and on our lettuce, a lapse in communication leading to fatalities. The group making this decision told me they had been hypervigilant, hypersensitive, and terrified by the possibility of offending respected leaders.

The Medical Device Industry is swimming in the culture of harm. By placing devices on a fast-track for approval, transplants are often deep in human tissue prior to full testing and market approval. Thousands of patients made it off the donor-recipient list only to find themselves on a recall list. The device failed or the original product was never approved, leaving thousands suffering from a serious threat. Not an opinion, but a well-documented fact pattern.

Those selling landscaping equipment have hidden their fatal flaws leading to multiple fatalities. Home-medical providers remained quiet in the case of defective and lethal dialysis products. The Mental Health community chose to stay dumb in the case of mood stabilizing medications that had the opposite impact, also leading to casualties. We find the lack of openness over many years in faulty appliances, problematic construction gear, and log splitters that turn on their handler. And many will remember those offenders who promoted leaking breast implants.

"90% of Registered Nurses surveyed admit to remaining silent; avoiding a crucial conversation with a physician even when they know a patient's safety may be at risk."

-Harvard Business Review, David Maxwell, December 7, 2016.

In far too many cases, investigators refer to the mechanical or physical failure leading to harm. Blaming equipment, product or defects the most popular, only to discover the human decision to apply or hide the flaw is the actual cause of predictable harm. We find the evidence, and I make the point by sharing the miscommunication and deliberate silence in the presence of a known threat before the 1986 Space Shuttle Challenger accident. The space shuttle, part of a comeback and PR campaign, had been delayed many times, adding to increased stress, diminished logic, and eventually a flawed decision. The Challenger exploded as it reached 46,000 feet and 73 seconds after liftoff, killing all on board. Aerospace subcontractors and the experts manufacturing the product told NASA leaders freezing weather could create extreme impacts to "O-Rings" and lead to an explosion. NASA leaders responded with a flurry of telephonic meetings, and the manufacturer eventually softened their stance.

Mid-managers and others on the Mission Control team were kept in the dark or muzzled before the "Go-Launch" sequence. I had a meaningful exchange with an insider close to the company manufacturing the O-ring. He reported the warning was issued, the shuttle would "blow-up" if launched in the near-freezing temperature. He believes placing public image over safety in the face of predictable and preventable danger killed the crew.

Thousands of students and small children had tuned-in, including the entire student body of Concord High School, Concord, Ohio. Concord High was wired-in via direct NASA feed, proudly watching an award-winning teacher Christa McAuliffe, 37, who joined the crew and the glory of one minute, thirteen seconds of flight. Instead of celebrating, the children, now adults, are forever stuck with the mental imagery of the teacher's violent death. To date, the historical record generated by NASA supports accidental explosion as the cause of death. True; however, human errors and decisions preceded a preventable explosion, another case of side-stepping responsibility, and our willingness to allow incomplete facts in the scrolls of time.

Cultural Change

While reasons vary, human communication related to real threats continues to fade. We are noticing the danger, but we either blow it off or move on to a fresh distraction. Research points to overwhelming data, distractions, and fear of rejection (addressed in chapter three). Evidence points to confusion, panic, or a total disconnection when it comes to a known threat leading to tragedy. Many have asked for the standard, the moment we know a culture is sliding toward becoming a delinquent subculture. We have a definition crafted by a workgroup with a diverse background. I've always enjoyed pragmatic definitions. The training group came up with a sound, topic-related meaning.

What is Considered Harmful?

"A harmful subculture, discussed during meetings and training, includes a threshold. The cultural crisis consists of any group or organization omitting facts, not sharing threats, or denying a threat exists in the face of overwhelming evidence to the contrary. The culture or attitude often includes two extremes: 1) Fear intensifies to the point of panic, or 2) disconnection. Both are barriers to communication, the missing ingredient in preventing accidental and intentional harm (Figure 2)."

2017: The Year of Meaningful Lessons

In our history of unfortunate silence and flawed reasoning, each contributing case begged for communication as trusted professionals dodged, delayed, and withheld information after the threat was known. Like Lady Concordia, the stated cause was not the root-cause. We are quick to find faulty equipment, flawed policy, O-Rings, and a so-called unforeseen "process-flaw" as the guilty party. The fictitious blame leads the news story as if humans were nowhere near the tragedy.

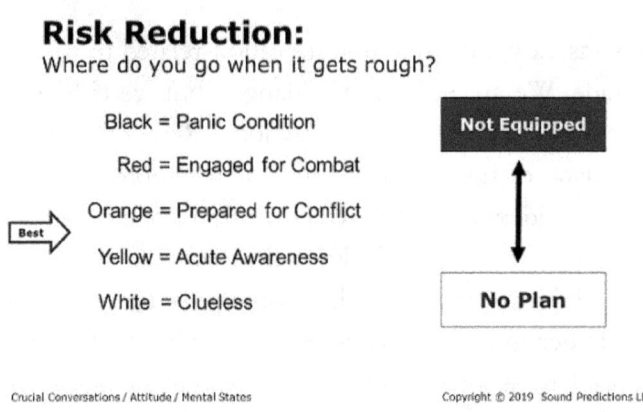

Figure 2: Addresses overwhelm; the impact of stress on problem-solving and crucial conversations. Panic on the high-end, disconnection on the low. Participants are asked to select an appropriate state of awareness for themselves.

Human behaviors are consistently the cause, and a second-sin found in our resistance to share the danger and or soften the facts. Relaxing the reported cause of death is usually done out-of-respect. The murky facts, however, also impact the timely reduction of risk and future incidents. The cases outlined or investigated for this text are not murky, confusing or questionable. We are talking about known threats followed by half-hearted efforts to curb the outcome. The historical pattern, developing over the past four decades, would reach an unfortunate climax in 2017.

By examining a 40-year pattern of intentional and not-so-obvious hazards, danger, and threats, a cultural norm becomes clear. The theory became undeniable in 2017. As a culture, we often recognized the risk and warning signs, but the same culture supported silence. In many cases, the bad guy verbalized a specific intention to kill. Our response? Silence! Mass casualty crimes in 2017 included those with information that could have prevented the incident. They chose silence until after the episode. Yes, they came forward and stated the bad guy had told them of his intention before he committed the homicides. While the cause and rationale vary, silence or flawed communication appeared as the frequent and fatal flaw. The culture, albeit innocently, had supported saying nothing when a few words would save a life. While a fictional social media message may traverse the globe in minutes, we struggle with the communication needed to prevent true casualties.

Not Convinced?

The numbers and official reports are difficult to deny. In examining the most dramatic and intentional acts of 2017, we discover disturbing facts. Again, and according to the most credible source, the FBI Behavioral Science Unit, over 50% of the mass shootings in 2017 involved a shooter who specifically told another person of the intention to kill before the act. Further shocking the senses, the witness did not report the threat. The plan to murder innocent people was known, and a capable and sane witness did nothing. The scenario repeated in over half of the active-shooter assaults and homicides in 2017. A trail of murder victims, completed acts, with open admission to knowing the plan yet doing nothing, affirm the cultural crescendo. We will revisit the specific FBI study, more details, and positive suggestions later in the book.

Cultural Shift

We can encourage safety ability and confidence while protecting our decisions with the armor of defensibility. Every suggestion and environmental clue defined in this text is defensible within the proper context. The evidence continues to build, supporting the need for quality assessments and prompt communication. Rejecting our innate ability to judge a threat followed by remaining silent is not working. Avoiding personal injury, damage, loss of reputation and brand, and protecting who and what we love, begins with the courage to see, judge and express concern.

"Failure to have the crucial conversation leads to loss; CEO's report losing up to 25% of their 'good employees' because they avoided the necessary conversation with a single problem-employee."

-Harvard Business Review Online, 2016.

The process outlined in this text, and material currently delivered during our training process, needs rapid communication. The problematic lesson comes from recent history. We genuinely need to encourage rather than find guilty those who share the possible threat, even when the opinion isn't correct. Predicting harm is a developing science. We must get beyond our hypervigilance for correctness for the process to continue. We expect to see errors, miscalculations, and mistakes during the learning process. We learn by trial and error; mistakes in the pursuit of stopping an act or accident is evidence of being wrong for all the right reasons. The honorable errors include those made as we try to protect kids, schools, churches, gay nightclubs, employees, and most important, our immediate families. Mistakes made in the pursuit of predicting and preventing harm deserve commendation, not condemnation.

The Sixth-Sense is Optional

Predicting harm does not call for a sixth-sense, but effectiveness needs courage, training, practice, error, much discussion, and more practice. This form of risk-reduction and the discipline of forecasting has and will continue to save lives, money, and time while lowering frustration, on and off the job. I don't intend to minimize the task before us; it is a significant cultural shift to elevate the role of The Predictor as a social and safety norm. The facts, however, point to a collision of hypersensitivity and the need for more communication. The rapid communication needed to improve safety, is a real challenge supporting the call for a refreshed safety strategy.

Feed & Fertilize Existing Skills

Prediction power is a mindset, part of our human capacity, a priceless gift just waiting to be fed and nurtured. Modern times, over-reliance on policy, a sense of security, weapons, and equipment, have tempted us away from the peaceful discipline. We often do not refine and enlarge the skill-set supporting the innate ability to foresee harm. Not a matter of blaming, but the current conversation in North America and beyond, vacillates and leads to atrophy. New generations have been raised to be less fearful for a good reason, but we may have overshot the mark. My research points to overconfidence in street safety and a form of Tombstone Courage on the job, both a potential barrier to cultural change. With less of a need to sharpen the saw of awareness and safety many never consider the art of prediction and prevention. Some, including me, are forced to adapt and improve safety-skill due to circumstances, neighborhoods, domestic violence, and those unstable situations. Life explodes in front of us, pushing for our reaction or involvement.

QuikTip:

A mistake in judgment usually won't kill you, but too much fear about sharing your suspicions may be fatal.

Like many friends, I don't judge the world-of-risk for what it is but assess the world as I am. Safety becomes a matter of how I feel in my surroundings, rarely based on reality. The false sense of security often places us at-risk of harm in specific environments. Most North Americans and Western Europeans feel safe, and the skills of predicting injury and damage may have become flabby or uninteresting.

As most mothers would agree; we were born with the basics to forecast an injury-free day; we are wired to protect others and ourselves from both accidental and intentional harm. Being wired for skills does not guarantee a sense of duty; to listen, act, share or enlarge the discipline. But daily communication certainly moves the needle to the positive. Dialogue is still our number one barrier, and I found it in many cases of preventable violence, silly assumptions, and avoidable accidents. I leave it up to readers, leaders, and students to weigh their obligation; to refine, respond to, or ignore safety needs. The thoughts, words, and actions suggested in this text are proven to reduce risk, but the art of forecasting harm and the necessary discipline remain an individual judgment call.

The article below, from USA Today (August 14, 2018), highlights the complexity of the threat, recognition of warning signs, and the need for rapid communication. Is the article correct or questionable? Does the story create panic or is it considered over-reporting? Does the article promote good awareness or culture on the cusp of change? I leave it up to you.

Headline: There were nearly 1,300 more threats made at U.S. schools this past year, report finds. - Marina Pitofsky, USA Today

"Violent incidents in schools increased 113 percent during the past school year, a new study finds. Schools saw 279 violent incidents during the 2017-18 school year, up from 131 the previous year, according to a survey by the Educator's School Safety Network, a national non-profit school safety organization.

The study, released Aug. 6, 2018, found that the most frequent violent incident was seeing a gun on campus, followed by shootings and thwarted attacks. The study also saw an increase in threats of violence in schools across the country, with nearly 1,300 more threats made during the current school year compared with last year.

The uptick can't be traced back to a single cause, according to Amy Klinger, director of programs at the Educator's School Safety Network and co-author of the report. She said the primary reason schools are seeing an increase in violence is because not enough preventive action is taken until it's too late. "We're waiting until things are so bad that we have a perpetrator with a gun before we do something," Klinger said. "If they (teachers) do have training, it's in active shooter response. It's not in violence prevention, threat-assessment or being able to identify and intervene with individuals of concern."

In March, the House passed the STOP School Violence Act to give over $1 Billion to schools and local governments over the next decade for violence prevention. The money would be used for metal detectors and other tools and programs. Doctor Drew Barzman, a child forensic psychiatrist at Cincinnati Children's Hospital Medical Center, said training teachers on warning signs in students is critical to keep schools safe. Barzman said warning signs can range from subtle behavior changes, like becoming withdrawn, to making threats against teachers and fellow students. "I don't think teachers know, off hand, what to look for right now," Barzman said. "That's something we can educate teachers about."

Parkland's Complicated Legacy

The report found that 27 percent of the violent incidents in the current school year have happened since the Valentine's Day shooting at Marjory Stoneman Douglas High School, which left 17 dead. In the 30 days following the Feb. 14 shooting at Marjory Stoneman Douglas, 35 percent of threats for the entire school year occurred, as did 27 percent of all violent incidents, according to the report. But Klinger said the Parkland shooting isn't solely to blame for the rise in violent incidents during the school year. Between fall

2016 and fall 2017, before the shooting itself, violence in schools had already increased 60 percent. In fall 2017, there were 90 acts of violence committed at schools, including shootings on the Rancho Tehama Reserve in California and Freeman High School in Rockford, Washington.

Parkland points to a greater problem in schools around the United States, Klinger said. "Parkland was not a catalyst for the increase, but a symptom of the overall increase. It's oversimplifying to say, 'Parkland happened, and therefore you have a 113 percent increase in incidents of violence,'" Klinger said. "There was an increase already in the works."

The Parkland shooting has a more direct correlation with the increase in threats of violence, according to Klinger. She said high-profile shootings make people more willing to report guns on campuses or threats against schools. Students are rarely unaware of high-profile acts of violence like the Parkland shooting, Barzman said. "They all know about it," Barzman said. "Confusion is one common theme. So is being really scared and not really knowing what to think."

However, Klinger said that heightened awareness due to the Parkland shooting still cannot account for the increase in violence schools saw in the fall semester. Factors ranging from access to weapons to a lack of school preparedness all played a part in the uptick. "That's what I think is so frustrating about school safety in general," Klinger said. "There are no easy answers or quick fixes."

End of Chapter Two

CHAPTER THREE

Victim Mindset: A Temporary Condition

Chapter three dives into the mind, thought-patterns, and the temporary attitude found in victim-thinking. Criminology studies the subculture leading to intentional harm, public safety addresses vehicle accidents, and industrial safety examines workplace hazards. Forecasting harm lowers risk in all three environments, which include a victim thought process. This chapter we'll take a good look at vulnerability by examining a bad mood called victim-thinking.

This short tour will not promote specific weapons or how to build a residential bunker. The survival stories are presented later, and I have no intention to distract you with another debate. We will visit the ideal mental-track for safety, health, and longevity. Once again, we'll side-step changing the world. Chapter three offers a partial remedy wholly reliant on the individual attitude. The thought-process may spread to the family and workgroup, lowering injury, damage and loss. But a lifesaving mindset starts with you and goes nowhere without your help.

The healthy environment, one embracing the realities of predictable harm, will consider two tracks:

1) Understanding the habits and intentions of a primitive

offender, and

2) The truth about victim-vulnerability, which eventually visits every individual, community, and environment.

While the examination of the offender is more interesting, getting a grip on victim-vulnerability will save more lives. The research of those at-risk has changed assumptions of the past. There is no *victim* personality type. Victims do not fit into a permanent profile as the victim-mindset may come and go. Defining the characteristics of a victim-mindset are part of the educational process and understanding your exposure, the present vulnerability, should be given priority.

Proof is Found in our Patterns

As an educator, I've found that any recurring and destructive pattern flags a need for a fresh strategy. Once the pattern is fixed at the individual, workgroup, corporate, or community level it rarely self-corrects. We can argue, fight to be right, and defend the status quo, but the stats have no agenda. The fact remains any pattern of behavior or performance ending negatively calls for intervention and leadership. And we never have a group of volunteers begging for the job. Chapter three aims to refine the process. Safety begins with a decision to use the mind more effectively in interrupting patterns. The full-awareness of a victim-mindset is where we begin; staying safe in the current moment, and enjoying a peaceful evening or weekend, with or without being armed. We focus on how to stay focused, postponing the grand plan for the now-moment.

Strategic policy and active protection rarely share center-stage. We must have certainty in the present-moment to predict and prevent harm. My research points to cases of injury and death where those focused-on policies may have missed the clues and cues of the present risk. Standard operating procedures are still essential but work in a different time zone. Applied incorrectly, policy can be a problem in the avoidance of a violent confrontation. In some cases, irrational rules may even interfere with the intuitive sense.

Know Your Scope

When policy, urgency, and corporate image are out-of-sequence, the distraction may lead to preoccupation; being mentally absorbed with administration can be a distraction. The fact remains, any disconnection from the present threat increases vulnerability. Periods of high conflict also enlarge the problem. Chronic distress should never be considered the norm. Weakened teams and individuals are off-the-risk-chart when stewing in long-term strife and misery, which change logic and reasoning. Not part of the time and not occasionally, risk of harm is elevated every time we get stuck in the cycle of dispute. Discussing distant goals, strategic plans, and frustrations while addressing a real threat is dangerous. It blurs the lines of ownership and responsibility. We numb-the-norm, and norming is the required foundation for forecasting harm. We often set-up the conditions for missing cues and clues of danger. The line of thinking is difficult to believe but statistically supported; I've been present for the debacle.

In one case a well-meaning police administrator interrupted a crucial conversation to discuss overtime expenses. It was imperative to him; however, I politely asked if we could revisit the topic after we completed the task at hand. The task was an active and long-term negotiation with an armed and barricaded suspect. Bad guys with guns, active engagement, a need for sequential focus, and the boss wants to check-in on overtime costs for the incident.

Wildly distracting, the behavior by a leader is not unusual, horrible or surprising. In this case, the boss was not malicious, selfish or thoughtless; he was sitting outside of the negotiations van reviewing records. Crunching numbers with his calculator and stressed by the costs, he opened the door and blurted out his concern. Managing expense is valid and within his scope. Protecting the negotiation, sequence, and process is within mine. Highlighting the boundary for the boss, and verbally separating our roles fell to me. Avoiding the victim-trap includes known boundary lines and refreshing it as needed. Victim vulnerability often flares up when the lines are unclear or not verbalized.

The Victim-Trap

The term victim is overused in some areas, avoided altogether in others, and misunderstood in most environments. We need to spend a moment developing a standard definition and a useful template. When we understand the victim-mindset, we know how to recognize it in ourselves and others. As we avoid getting stuck in the modern mental state, we are free to make the rapid decisions needed for predicting and sidestepping harm. Our limbs, lives, and our professional reputation rely on focus. The rational delay of misplaced thoughts and self-destructive victimhood allow safe and prompt decisions.

Simple models help most women and men avoid the victim-trap as we crowd out distractions with simple models. While I encourage all students and participants in training to customize-as-needed, a 5-stage template has been well-received. As stress escalates our brilliant bodies stop, assess, and take the most familiar route. We have many examples of mental and muscle memory under the influence of pressure. Children trained in a floor exercise or dance routine begin the practice when they hear familiar music in not-so-familiar surroundings. It may be in the mall, church or a waiting room; when the music sounds familiar, they start the dance. In the adult world, we see the sequential in morning habits, martial arts, and driving a car. We react because we have trained, considered, and practiced a sequence we can rely upon without significant effort or conscious thought.

The five dimensions of forecasting harm offer a sequential habit. Once trained, considered, and attached to your routine, the process leading to a forecast should become a fixed part of the mind. Interruptions will occur, the resulting anger, broken sequence, and fatigue only threaten the solution and our ability to problem-solve. Plus, our pressures and worry out of sequence with reality also contribute to casualties. The new hazards and an increasingly busy world call for common language. The partial solution is found in a template promoting focus and process; when to predict, when to act, when to retreat. The five dimensions of predictable harm, a process I first developed for schools and public transit, offers a starting point.

Examining violence and accidents, we found five common threads of weakened awareness. Interviews and documentation included sources considered victims, witnesses, and those closest to the deceased at the time of the event. Initially, I had sought common environmental elements of vehicle accidents and assaults. I was surprised to find defensible evidence specific to victims and related interruptions. In the majority of these cases, the casualty had compromised awareness around clues and cues, reduced communication, and was often in a work culture suffering a lack of shared-risk. Incorporating the assistance of clients, colleagues, and unpaid volunteers, we reviewed nearly 4000 cases with a known victim. We recorded data from actual reports and followed-up with live interviews in 25%, or 1000 cases. Most of our R&D group did not like what the findings revealed. We eventually concluded most of the cases were entirely avoidable. The project shifted from data mining to education, and that brings us to No Further Harm, the educational journey and this text.

Beyond training and development, I rely on the template to ensure a clean estimation of danger. I suggest capturing the five stages in writing, memorialize the lesson on a laminated card, and carry the reminder or display the refresher on the mirror or bulletin board. The five stages are used for actual applications, debriefing a near-miss, court testimony or as a shift orientation starting. They lower the concerns of leadership, and add credibility to a presentation or explanation:

1. NORMING: Identification and understanding a stable norm; the safe, comfortable environment you consider within acceptable standards of safety. Norming is the baseline needed for correct predictions, judgment, and positive assessment.

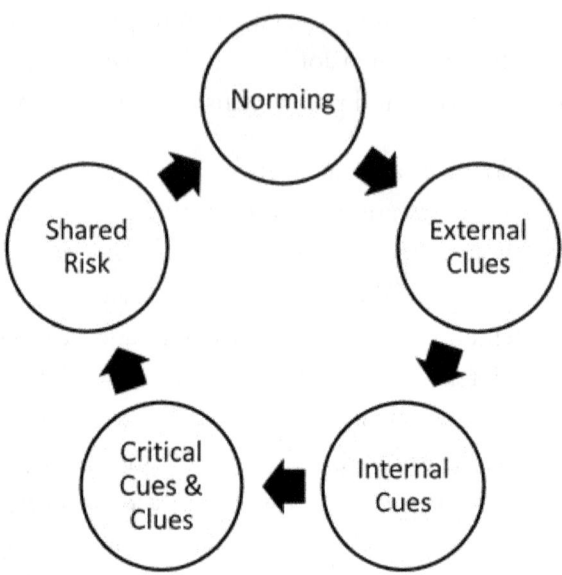

2. EXTERNAL CLUES: Useful or unusual evidence calling for more information; the hint of danger, equipment, external signals, and clues that deviate from, or threaten the norm,

3. INTERNAL CUES: Internal reactions or warning signs out-of-balance with individual norms. The gut-check, intuitive sense, or change from the normal, internal condition. The internal-atmosphere includes our natural intuition drowning in distractions. Regardless of facts, internal deviations call for your attention (it doesn't feel right, the small voice, or signal suggesting a pause or a full-stop),

4. CRITICAL OR STAND-ALONE EVIDENCE: A single warning sign (clue) or internal reaction (cue) making no other evidence necessary. Critical evidence, undeniable threats, weapons, violent conditions, or illness. Any impactful condition or injury, or a key team member missing may qualify as a stand-alone (critical cue or clue), and

5. SHARED RISK (Rapid Communication): This includes weighing the need for and acting on a rapid communication strategy. Knowing with whom, when, and why it calls for immediate communication. Timely communication is the missing element in many visible accidents and acts of violence over the past 72 months. Who is your first point of contact as you raise the alarm? Is there a timeline for rapid communication? Most important, do they have permission and a sense of urgency in communicating concerns? Once shared, we ask for feedback. Do they understand which people, topics, and what sets up urgency? Does it include a phone call to the boss in the middle of the night? Do they know to call police before the boss? The last point being a major contributor to deadly delays.

Again, the five dimensions illustrate vulnerabilities; one or more preventative measures missing prior to an accident or intentional harm, such as workplace violence. Most casualties over the past 72-months, included missed opportunities in one or more forecasting dimensions. Because they represent five dimensions of vulnerability, they become five training objectives.

Risk Reduction via the Five Dimensions

On the contrary, and in one form or another, each of the five dimensions are present in most success stories; accidents and intentional acts avoided. To date, two stages offer a challenge and urgency. Internal Cues (intuitive cues or dimension #3), and Shared Risk (rapid communication; with who, when, and what to share, or dimension #5). I found the two were deficient in most needless injuries, losses, and fatalities. Ignoring intuition or saying nothing about a threat we can no longer ignore, lead the race in failed interventions. Again, I don't emphasize patterns to ridicule past behaviors leading to injury or resulting in death; they are amplified to prevent similar actions and highlight teachable moments in the chain of events. Some incidents and accidents, and most mass shootings over the past 72-months could have been prevented if internal cues had been respected and clues shared rapidly.

Best practices (and the worst) are highly contagious; the attitude will spread quickly, following favorable or dangerous direction. Small or grand, the culture of No Further Harm encourages prediction, immediate remedies in prevention, and is still available to those who follow a few simple guidelines. Most important, it starts with the individual decision to do it differently. It begins with you and dies without your approval.

When one commits in Good Faith to absorbing new knowledge around forecasting, I guarantee three outcomes: First, you will learn surprising facts about vulnerability, your exposure, and the high-risk, temporary mindset of others likely to become victims. Secondly, you will gain the upper hand in forecasting potential risk related to intentional harm, the accidental near-miss, and not-so-obvious criminal behaviors. Finally, once fully equipped with new risk-reduction information and environmental sensibilities, safety will be the natural result for you, and those within your scope of influence.

According to research by EHS.com, specialized in Environmental Health & Safety, literally 99% of our adverse events, incidents, and accidents are avoidable. Clues and cues present life-saving warnings to almost anyone following a few basic rules and deciding to end the numbness produced in the justification for risky and dangerous routines. Experts contributing to this text agree. The necessary and urgent conversation about risk is still elusive, politicized to the point of avoidance, and carefully sanitized.

Additionally, when it comes to the specific goal of violence reduction, our obsession with guns and gangs distracts us from the core issue of violence and the personal responsibility to reduce risk. The single-solution debate is exhausting; akin to blaming silverware for the culture of obesity. We can change obesity by locking the silverware drawer, but the social issues leading to cause will continue. Yes, we may temporarily reduce violence by cutting guns and gangs, but we're stuck with the true contributors found in a culture of violence. The full perspective cannot be addressed in one text as it includes thoughts, words, acts, musical lyrics, realistic games, upbringing, and entertainment. I've taken the route of education; narrowed the emphasis for this text to awareness, de-escalation, and prevention.

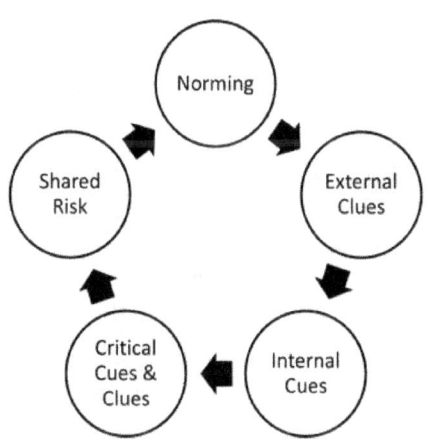

In the opinion of those much smarter than I, our current culture avoids the more prominent image and target of predictable harm by locking onto a single cause or solo cure. Those who run at the altitude of one-cause-single-cure thinking, are rarely conversational, often off-balance in matters of safety, and usually at higher risk of predictable violence and accidental injury. The fixed attitude interrupts healthy dialogue and cuts-off future conversation; suffering within a cycle of fighting and forgetting, we argue to the point of silence and ignore specific topics until the next act or accident. This topic of conversation will thread through the rest of the book. If we plan on reducing risk, we must take the struggle and sting out of life-saving conversations.

History: The Emerging Portrait of a Victim

Early in my first career, a 22-year assignment in public safety, victim-patterns, to include my own, began to surface. Accidents and graphic scene conditions began to form a template or pattern. In many cases, injury, error, and death shared common elements. Accident victims, suspicious crime scenes, mishaps in the home, and unfortunate carelessness began to cluster. The sketch, a blurry outline, eventually exposed trends. Common traits floated to the surface in many cases. While the human casualties had never met (numbering over 4000), their thoughts, words, attitudes, and behaviors lined up to form a temporary victim-profile.

These societal changes occurred in a community less connected, less likely to share observations, and unlikely to point out dangerous humans and the characteristics of their victims. During the adverse erosion of community relationships, a perfect storm began to develop. Public safety officials were promoting 9-1-1 communication systems, re-starting community policing efforts, and pushing special-emphasis units, which needed people, money, and intense media marketing. As a Police Public Information Officer during that time, I was immersed in the strategy, a strong and innocent push for the use of government services.

QuikTip:

"A verbal or written threat changes the rules as safety concerns exceed the need for confidentiality."

While unintentional, we convinced the public to disengage, stay safe, continue to Just Say No, and call 9-1-1. The message contributed to a feeling of safety and comfort, and the illusion that public safety has your back, 24 hours, seven days a week. The subtle message encouraged the public to dial 9-1-1 for everything from a burglary to a child who refuses to go to bed. The Call-4-Anything culture was smooth sailing for a few years until the system became saturated with the explosion of 9-1-1 calls. 65% increase in low need, non-priority calls peaked, compounded by crime due to the crack cocaine epidemic.

The Perfect Storm

No Further Harm: A Purely Predictable Path

In-between reports of 'shots fired' and service calls requesting a mountain pass report, 9-1-1 was called to report sprinklers recklessly shooting over a property line and hitting the caller's deck. Uniformed officers responded to investigate Cedar planks, legally entitled to a dry day, and under attack by unwanted water. 9-1-1 calls increased for true violence along with the nuisance calls of smoke from a BBQ. Peace Officers with bulletproof vests investigated the fatty-steak-fumes wafting into the innocent ventilation system of a community member. Without question, the unwarranted trauma guaranteed a two-car response. My favorite example of all-things-urgent included a police response about a hard-working woman changing her oil late at night. When told it was not unlawful to change oil at 10:24 PM, the caller increased the urgency by claiming "She's very dangerous, packs a weapon, and will probably dispose of the oil illegally." Public safety professionals sent two cars, a total of three officers to service the call. The officers carefully scoped-out the possibility of a future crime; a woman that may be conspiring to dispose of 4.5 quarts of 10-40 weight motor oil illegally. I realize it was important, but not most important! Frequently the case, the caller and the woman changing her oil had never met.

Government services and the 9-1-1 abuse, rightly earned, created a wave we never expected, at a price society is still paying at the time of this publication. We created a codependent public within individual communities, unreasonable expectations in others, and influenced the masses to disengage. We discouraged healthy dialogue in our effort to gain the needed love from our communities. We also discouraged discussions with risky people or during risky conflicts but forgot to describe or define a level of risk the community is expected to address without the police. The children witnessing a changing culture, exposed to a risk-adverse system, are now our employees, teachers, safety reps, and our top leaders.

Systemic Distractions

Atrophy developed in the human muscle used to tactfully diffuse risk and rage. While nations convinced children to battle drugs and promoted Just Say No, the police and sheriff created an overburdened police culture that couldn't say no. Promising and delivering 110% service created a lasting impact; the powerful message that there is no need to forecast harm or practice vigilance. We no longer required connectedness or the personal responsibility to predict and prevent damage through healthy communication, minus the authority. The evidence is found in the injury and death, documented accidents, and acts of violence over the past 72 months and beyond.

The New Victim Profile

In most casualties, the term "victim" is used to define unfortunate individuals, and each victim usually has a name. For this text, I removed the names, gender, race, geographical location, and I often ignore the profession or living arrangements. The tags and identifiers become dangerous icons that allow us to exclude or minimize our own risk; i.e., 'I'm not a Mail Carrier. I'll never get bit by a nasty dog.' Or, 'I don't work in construction. Falling debris, electrocution, and confined spaces do not relate to me.' Or 'I live by myself. I do not need conflict communication or de-escalation skills.' I relied on multiple organizations to broaden the victim-footprint; however, carefully avoided offering a specific victim landscape or occupation.

With the help of key contacts within each industry, I narrowed the focus to thoughts, words, actions; an honorable mention reserved for poor choices or behaviors. The reality would eventually highlight a temporary attitude and vulnerable mindset; the passing condition, which doesn't have an accident, injury, or sexual assault history. VICTIM is no-longer a label but a state of mind.

We've learned that harm seeks a temporary host. Tragic and preventable acts often seek the common carrier of industry,

No Further Harm: A Purely Predictable Path

community, workgroup, family or the individual who slipped into the temporary mindset. The key word is *temporary*. Some victims studied and interviewed had been recently transferred, were new

to the community, running new equipment, newly hired or lost in a new region. All the above, once blended with a missed clue or cue of danger, closed the cycle with an injury or death. In most of these mainstream cases, I found a rough template. Most injuries, accidents, and intentional acts included victims wandering into harm's way, stumbling into predictably risky situations, and those who knew better. When I examined the history of the victim some had not been injured on the job, and no vehicular accidents off the job. They were often suffering from innocent distractions, passing illnesses, or Tombstone Courage (poor judgment wearing the mask of bravery). They had entered a dangerous environment, in many cases, a situation that never changed; however, the internal conditions of the victim temporarily altered.

Invert the pattern of vulnerability, and we discover a positive and empowering course of instruction we can teach, discuss, and apply to interrupt fixed cycles of harm. Once aware, I no longer believed in a life sentence for victims, dangerous neighborhoods, and a permanent punishment for the temporarily unsafe. My research supports the temporary condition, temporary vulnerability that may be amended and made whole, secure, and safer than ever.

The list of ingredients leading to unnecessary and elevated risk is lengthy and includes both positive attributes and harmful components. Distractions include recent losses, disagreements, audits, and the common cold. Positive anticipation also shows up as a distraction - a new home, a newly constructed hip, and a new love interest. Some casualties had won big money at the casino, from an investment or a court settlement, others had losses. Some victims of violence and injury had recently started a medical procedure, and others stopped medications against medical advice. Some had started a relationship with the undiagnosed or unknown predator. Almost every case of intentional or accidental harm includes vulnerability in the form of temporary conditions.

Historically, we have blamed external conditions for our demise or casualty, while the real culprit is an inside issue with lousy timing, vulnerability meeting danger. The solution involves recognizing not only the symbolic shiny coin stealing our attention but the specific and elevated risk presently inside of us. Harm is miserably ineffective without the opportunity to act. Our attitude often presents the opening, the open-door surrenders the home court advantage to our adversary, which is the unchecked danger.

Like many of my colleagues, I had been in love with a fixed-science focused on security, witnesses, bad-guys, protective equipment, the bizarre, abnormal mind of deviants, and the standard VICTIM. We love a safe and stable definition as we examine the social underbelly. Hollywood loves it too. I was mesmerized by the urgency and the human and inhumane acts in the middle of the night. I still enjoy the examination of those appearing normal while planning the disgusting acts of predation. But you; the reader, the community, and the viewers only get a headline. The drama or a few 30-second clips of a publicized trial never supplied the full-meal-deal. The entertainment platform never allows a continuous feed of preventative advice; information we can use to judge the workplace trauma, the loss of a finger, or the violent act. Most of all, we rarely discuss and define the VICTIM.

I decided to author a book about victimology only after I interviewed those who blamed victims and after reading reams of reports. Curiosity led me to meetings with safety officers and those who occupy the skies, oceans, and corporate high-rises. I was surprised by the widespread opinion that threats and vulnerability are somehow unique to a profession, poverty-level or location. Misconceptions are present across a broad spectrum of jobs, volunteer positions, those who work at home, make our laws, and some who lead our communities. The facts and history of harm offer contrary facts.

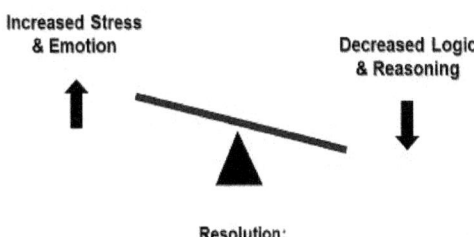

Except for spontaneous disasters, the victim-footprint includes a temporary victim mindset. The brief offering or sacrifice is usually an innocent lapse. Lasting a moment, and generally without a near miss, injury or fatality. Eventually, the unchecked errors become the habit. Our pattern, rarely interrupted by reality, is often misidentified as a victim personality.

Dangerous Silence

Habitually intrigued by the dramatic elements of industry and personal risk, I was surprised by the limitations of public debate and lack of genuine solutions. The two extremes of highly academic discourse (limited by experience) and barbaric solutions (limited by brain function) include little action. We often avoid the awkward performance-zone of prevention; risk created by our habits, failures, ignorance, silence, and innocent vulnerability. The temporary victim-mindset is often felt, but rarely shared. We have everything we need to safeguard the young and most vulnerable in a stable society. We have the tools, the eyes, the concerns, and we have the science. Missing is life-saving communication and the courage to share what we see in our potential or temporary victims.

Victimology is available, and I believe we are compelled to share ethically, legally, and morally. These temporary risk factors offer solutions; victimhood moves beyond the weakest individual; the temporary mood or state often changes the fit, the powerful, and the affluent. Being a victim is not a life-goal, an impossibility or a permanent sentence. The definition used in our formal training classes, crafted and vetted by a diverse group of adults, is straightforward:

Victim Mindset Defined: *A temporary mood, attitude or state of mind; a predictable, natural, and emotional condition resulting from external events and internal reactions; with the intensity to interrupt safe, sequential habits and routines. Victim-Mindset includes any thoughts or behaviors that discount or interfere with the recognition of present risks, danger signs, and a potentially hazardous environment.*

I once believed injury and harm struck without an appointment and with no time for preparation. Victimhood was a random curse striking the unfortunate soul in life's lottery. I also visited the other end of the victim-spectrum; a theory those struck down in the prime of life stood for a victim branded by deliberate lifestyle and choice. 'Street thug, addict, homeless, and the woefully out-of-touch' were high-risk victims the media refused to define. I've tempered that opinion while keeping the notion as correct, on a much smaller scale. I was forced to re-evaluate my worldview after seeing a life-threatening incident that included an avoidable mistake on the job. Like many cases of accidental loss, injury, and death, it seemed spontaneous. The case involved a drug-addicted driver who became a life-long felon after a split-second decision and a six-second crime spree. The grave set of circumstances unfolded on a city street, leading to temporary injuries, intentional self-defense, mandatory reports, and preparation for a courtroom drama. The impetus for this book lasted only seconds, leaving powerful lessons spanning over decades. A thorough review of the event became the keystone in the construction of a pattern we will discuss in detail; the value of knowing the victim profile and how we can reduce exposure or avoid the template altogether.

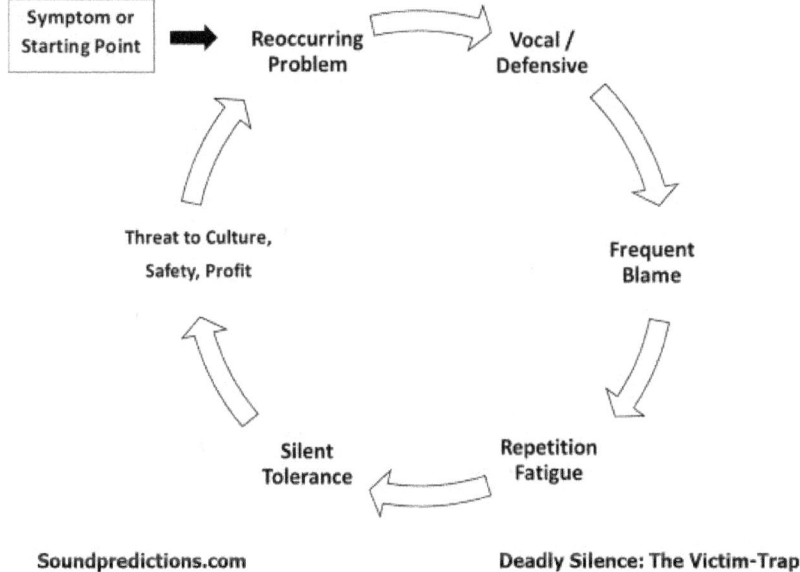

Figure 3: Illustrates the cycle of reoccurring conflicts and injury. Also called **Fight & Forget**, the cyclic leads to frustration, malicious compliance, and eventually fatigue and silent tolerance; many leaders believe the problem has gone away but it only went underground. Inevitable loss, injury or fatality regenerates the cycle. The temporary victim-mindset is found in silent tolerance.

The details, shared in chapter five, will clarify how Adrenaline impacts judgment, amplifies assumptions and may lead to mistakes. The story had a purpose, and when victims have meaning, they rarely get stuck in the victim mindset. While I'm not suggesting a training sermon at the bedside of injured loved ones, lessons often over-ride the silent suffering found in victim regret. Those injured by accidents or assault often find comfort in sharing their story as a qualified expert in survival. Once recovery is underway, we should privately ask every victim if they would like to share their story.

End of Chapter Three

CHAPTER FOUR

Distraction and Vulnerability

While the conversation is never easy, the evidence found in recent history begs for closer look and more dialogue. Safe habits and reduced vulnerability start with dialogue. The proof is in the credentials of new patterns, an increase in standard errors, and a list of new causes. The Costa Concordia tragedy offers one example; distraction and conflict are not new but tuning-out with a 'dank' round of PlayStation or Sega Heroes while running a massive cruise ship indeed are. The question is how we address vulnerability created by and through distractions. Chapter four will examine the reality of distractions, the death of the  multi-tasking myth, and why the solution must include leadership.

Like the crucial conversations needed but missing or delayed in over 50% of the mass shootings in 2017, chapter four supplies the evidence of dangerous distractions or delays before severe and fatal accidents. Some believe the correlation is flawed science, that is until they review the data. Increased and unmanaged stress, conflict and interruptions lead to poor communication, and flawed dialogue in losses, injuries and fatalities. The research related to a 72-month fact-pattern is undeniable. The world has become a noisy place. The adjustment may need a new perspective on old experiences, and hopefully, chapter four will convince you that managing distractions reduces harm.

Our ability to focus is never completely gone, but may fade from lack of use, a new obsession, or a temporary illness. The evidence often presents itself in minor conflicts and eventually dramatic consequences. Small errors and other signals tell us when we're losing our edge in driving, jogging, operating equipment, general awareness, and how we conduct ourselves during difficult conversations. The small stressors or conflicts, often ignored or blamed on others, are a gift to those who pay attention. We can awaken our focus and re-master the art of awareness in a reasonably short timeframe, however, rarely do so without symptoms or pain.

Head-on collisions, running over a child, getting fired or divorced, and sinking a cruise ship are the unnecessary extremes of distraction. Early-recognition and minor course-corrections are needed.

According to the Journal of Safety Research (ScienceDirect.com), motor vehicle accidents have skyrocketed for those under the age of 30. Distraction was the primary cause in nearly every case of a preventable, one-vehicle accident. Stated differently, we are injuring and killing ourselves with madness before we complete our 29th year. The one-car-rollover offers one of many examples pointing to interruption of the sequential process necessary in all-things-safety.

No Further Harm: A Purely Predictable Path

Fragmented due to interruptions and saturation of information, we are paying a high-price in the not-so-new e-world of hashtags, endless texting, and 24-hour disruptions. The paradox includes our increased need for rapid communication and the results of information overload. The experience of age-old urgency is not fresh, but why and how the pace creates elevated risk has changed.

A steady, uninterrupted stride has all but disappeared in our personal and professional lives, replaced by short sprints of work, and a quick-hit of e-completeness. We are often on and off-line with technology, interrupted by being on and off-task at work. Add the fact the multi-tasking is debunked; we find ourselves entering a dangerous intersection. I'm not criticizing changes in the availability of data but highlighting a distinct threat to safety in how we manage the process. With few exceptions, any potentially hazardous task becomes a potential fatality under the influence of distraction. Add job-task confidence or experience, and the risk of injury skyrockets under the false assumption of multitasking prowess and distraction. Much like an injury discussed in chapter five, the repetitive and dangerous task often creates a new-normal; adrenaline slows or stops, awareness fades, and risk moves off-the-chart. Like free-climbing a natural rock face for the seventh time, and just before leaving the plane for freefall number 500, confidence is helpful or hurtful. Poise and certainty are useful when we concentrate and remember the predictable harm before us.

Avoiding interruptions, visualizing or verbalizing a system of steps leading to safe execution, and then making it happen, completes a near-flawless sequence. According to experienced rock climbers, any interruption to the sequence creates danger and therefore considered off-limits. Veteran skydivers agree, if the safety chain necessary for the completion of a safe skydive has been threatened, they postpone the hazardous departure from the plane.

"A recent study by UC Irvine found the average office employee

gets interrupted every 11 minutes, and it takes an average of 25 minutes to return and focus on the original task." – NY Times, 2017

Those who lean to the extreme side of recreation shared a vital message when interviewed for the text: They manage distractions by managing themselves. They rely on simple rules, sharing the guidelines, and reinforcing the reason for constant focus. If internal or external disturbances are too high, they often self-select and do it another day, sidestepping risk. Self-discipline is the norm in the world of extreme sports, and if self-discipline erodes, peer-coaching steps up to fill the vacancy. The professional environment doesn't always offer the opportunity for choice, but we engage others whenever possible.

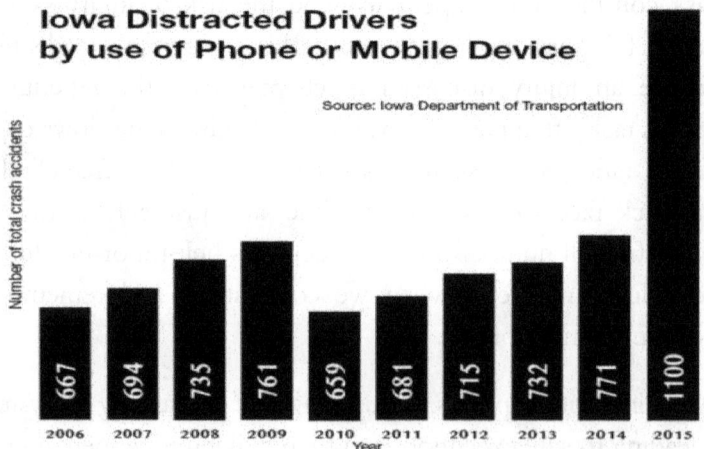

The Multi-Tasking Fable

The not-so-ancient tale of multi-tasking lures both the young and old, a false belief they are the exception. Under the false assumption multi-tasking was a gift, I used to assign misaligned work-tasks and shoulder cockeyed responsibilities related to work.

Overseeing fleet mechanics while working at an educational facility forty miles away seemed doable at the time. It was messy, full of mistakes, and re-dos were the norm, doubling the risk of injury at 125% the cost.

The research has been sluggish; however, the data is starting to reach the user. While proven to increase the risk of harm and criminal victimization, some still believe it's possible to juggle daggers, change baby diapers, and interact on social media simultaneously. You may be the guilty party, or you know who they are. Haunted by a ghost of *I Know I Must Be Missing Something*, the hypervigilance and fulltime connectedness at superhuman speed leads to tragic results. The expectation of continuous information is not a problem, but collateral damage found in sustaining the pace is a formidable threat to safety.

In our pursuit of multi-tasking perfection, interpersonal conversations are often interrupted, sequential thinking becomes fragmented, simple tasks are started, and restarted again, which compromise safety. Predictable mistakes lead to the erosion of morale, quickly followed by small injuries, then casualties needing medical aid, and a financial hit to the employer and families. The saturation of data and our mistaken obligation to respond, add to an already busy life. Therefore, the loss of focus falls into the category of foreseeable harm; loss, injury, and the ultimate consequence of untimely death.

Work and Play

In many cases, the bright-lines separating work and play is nonexistent, leading to personal distractions on the job, and work-related distractions off-the-job. The cost continues to climb for individuals and employers who don't get it.

National Institutes of Health and University of California, Irvine, have done the homework:

1. According to UC Irvine, 80 percent of the student population report headaches, insomnia or eye twitch because of information overload, and they continue to return to the trough to consume more data,

2. 78% of all distracted motorists admit they were preoccupied with texting while driving,

3. Suspects in street crimes watch for victim vulnerability; distracted-by-technology tops their list (urban areas),

4. Over 330,000 recent accidents caused by distracted driving in 2017 resulted in severe injuries (severe defined as debilitating or life-changing),

5. Mobile-phone related injuries to pedestrians (trips, slips, and struck by vehicle) now exceed those for drivers, and

6. According to the Journal of Experimental Psychology, we double our error rates after a 2.8-second interruption, and errors triple after a 4.5-second distraction.

While injuries and harm on-the-clock re-documented, off-the-clock events are more difficult to track. The lessons learned from incidents in and near home offer compelling evidence of distractions. The list below, provided by our friends at the Center for Disease Control (CDC), supplies context and the top five. The home is typically our safe place, the zone of happiness and protection, and where we can drop our guard. Unfortunately, the home hides significant risks elevated due to familiarity and innocent distractions. More than 21,000 Americans die from predictable home-accidents each year, making our comfortable house the second-most-common location for casualties. Driving is the number one cause of a premature departure near the home.

According to the CDC, the five leading causes of unintentional home injury leading to death include:

A. Falls: Falling is the leading cause of accidental home fatalities; the only cause sharing an elevated position with work-related deaths. Falling at home claims nearly 9,000 lives per year. A fall from the roof is second to a fall in the tub or shower. The latter is woefully under-reported due to the nature of the event; challenging to admit for survivors, and rarely included on the death certificate as the cause. An uncertain environment and nothing to grab on the way to a solid surface contribute to the bathroom casualty.

B. Poisoning (including Rx): The second-leading cause of accidental home injury deaths—poisoning—takes nearly 7,000 lives each year. For young adults and the middle-aged, it's often the primary cause of unintentional death at home. We are rarely worried as we climb stairs, ladders, and into attics or crawl spaces at home. Overindulge or take a new prescription, decongestant, or potent but legal marijuana, and the simple task becomes a fatal fall due to toxicity. Plus, potentiation, the combination of drugs and alcohol, multiplies the risk of deadly accidents. Unintended access and consumption by our kids contribute; prescription drugs, over-the-counter meds and harmful household products.

C. Fire, smoke, and burns: Home fires and smoke inhalation claim more than 3,000 lives a year, making it the third-leading cause of accidental home injuries ending in death. Failure to practice escaping from the home and dead batteries in the detection system contribute to the cause.

D. Airway obstruction: Obstructed air passage, suffocation, and strangulation contribute to about 1,000 fatalities per year; young children being the primary victims. Blankets, marbles, the plastic eyes from a stuffed animal, and rolling into a suffocation position while sleeping, are often included in the details of a tragic loss.

E. Water-related harm: Submersion in water accounts for over 1000 deaths a year in the home. Again, water can be a peril to children, and it isn't always in the family pool. Some of the casualties

I reviewed included a bathtub with little standing water and a five-gallon paint bucket explored by the child. The child fell in, head first, and the bucket remained upright. In most cases of water-related harm, the investigation revealed no barrier or protective fence separating the young victims from the water.

A quick review of the tragic losses in the home category highlight two common threads:

1) Distractions cause 90% of the harm, and

2) The victim's deviation from the norm (reacting) contributed; rushing to complete a task or responding to a routine matter disguised as emergent (phone, text prompt, chime for a clothes dryer or washing machine). Attending to something as simple as a knock at the door, we innocently leave a child or disabled adult alone, or near the foreseeable hazard. Or, the distraction includes an unnecessary rush by the victim before death; trip, slip, or a fall while roofing, and trying to check that so-called important text message.

Stress, Hypervigilance, Too Many Tasks

My perspective about violence, accidents, and the role of distraction continue to evolve. Altered by new cases and useful information, not a week goes by without learning from experience or others relying on outdated myths. I enjoy a career trusting our rich history and abilities. Leadership and human performance under stress always produces new material. I examine and speak of the attitude, not because I'm proficient but due to my track record in full-time awareness. My past accident and error-rate were riddled with rushing, running late, and the failure to manage distractions. My trips to the emergency room, often prefaced by four words, were predictable. If a co-worker overheard me saying, "Sorry, I'm running late" or "Hey, watch this trick," an injury was probably in my immediate future. It would remain that way until I decided to manage my time, stress, and sense of urgency. Stated differently,

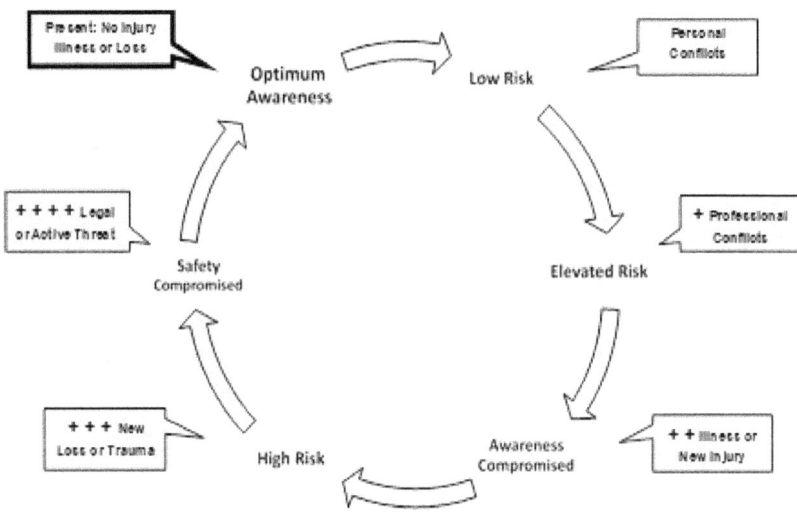

I chose to callout distractions instead of allowing distractions to control me. Stress management, communication, and awareness were not strong points in my early twenties. I was not always tuned-in to my surroundings, my responsibility to survive, and I rarely shared what I learned from my own mistakes. I was not the portrait of safety outlined in the text, but it changed.

QuikTip:

We rarely need to control others once we learn how to manage ourselves.

We each have the power to predict and enjoy the fruit of a safe day regardless of distractions. I don't promote avoidance as the only cure, but awareness of disturbance is the theme. This form of knowledge and ability is not due to intrigue or academic prowess. Lack of awareness nearly killed me, literally. I was forced to learn, accept, and grow through ignorance, injuries, and eventually research. I changed over time, and the complete safety overhaul now takes place each day. I start every day or hazardous task with a reminder, a prayer, and a mantra; *I'm not a victim but I'm not exempt.* I wholly believe the journey is an inside job but needs caring and direct observations from others.

Minimizing Mistakes & Maximizing the Lesson

Disorganization and a flawed sense-of-safety rarely announce their need for outside aid. Mistakes, injuries, and awkward attempts lead to lessons improving the entire safety landscape by reducing distraction. *No Further Harm* includes ending the lure of constant interruption; focus is the mantra for survival. The strong shift is also useful for those recovering from past errors and injuries, a point-of-focus serving those in the middle of a learning curve.

I find viewing history through the lens of predictability as educational, fun, and potentially life-sustaining. When I ask if an event was predictable, I'm not making an accusation, but setting myself up for continuous learning. If it was predictable, the next question relates to distraction. When we find the distraction, we have the next goal of training. I encourage every student and reader to maximize the educational value of mistakes, minor injuries, and those close calls through the filter of predictability; not only our missteps but the daily incidents we can now access in the age of information. I also look for and encourage others to find a healthy process currently underway and worthy of modeling.

The Negotiators

As I mentioned earlier, my current role in the private sector preceded two decades of public safety, responsible for a myriad of functions. Inner-city policing was a tough job; a world of predictable harm and distractions, where a hostile work environment was the norm instead of a rare complaint to HR. My duties included finding solutions related to cyclic patterns of harm, employee ability under stress, critical incident trauma, and motivating safe community mobilization. The highlight of public life included the role of Hostage Negotiator; ultimately promoted to Team Leader of our Crisis

No Further Harm: A Purely Predictable Path

Negotiations Unit in Washington State.

Every policy, new tactic, safety standard, and every innovation a negotiator enjoys, include a foundation of mistakes, those made by others and our own. This is a recommended standard found in every personal or professional safety system claiming success. In the flawed safety process or in cases of reoccurring problems, we see those who have not experienced failure. We also see those unable to maximize mistakes, their own and those within the industry or peer group.

Most crisis negotiators have developed the internal discipline and sidestep distractions. Through collective experience and fundamental human vulnerability, the negotiator can relate with offenders, victims, innocent bystanders, and members of the crisis team itself. Each negotiator on my side had survived a trauma, and most impacted as a victim of violence. I enjoyed the front-row seat in the adventure; however, it was not what most readers would guess or believe. I was granted a backstage pass into the lives of women and men who survived the storm and dedicated their lives to restoring peace in unstable and violent situations. My career-best and most difficult memories connect to crisis negotiations work. Our days included heroic and horrendous acts experienced by many on my team, and within the communities we served. Today, every past crisis and response hold value in my relationships, how and when I communicate, and in my contribution to this publication. I often look back, refreshing the lessons negotiators present and the process worth modeling.

To clarify how the negotiators managed crisis and distractions, we need to hit "pause" on the distorted Hollywood imagery floating through the mind. The job is nothing like the TV image; more technical than emotional, with a few career moments of life-changing violence. While serious when necessary, the team remained light-hearted most of the time. Real negotiators never work alone, never exchange a negotiator for a hostage, and we don't set up helicopters or buses to move a group of victim-hostages to a hideout in the hills. Negotiators craft and manage crucial conversations, shield the full SWAT team from distractions and simplify communications.

The role of a negotiator parallels the character of those navigating any crucial conversation; however, the process is clearly defined and sequential, reducing distractions by design. The shared attitude is predictive, focused on preventing harm, and needs an environment physically set-up to avoid distractions. Understanding how negotiators do it should be helpful; three vital functions reduce predictable damage and disturbance:

Responsibility Number One: Momentarily slow the process. We respond to emotional and tragic scenes where violence has occurred or is likely. As the scenario accelerates with reckless speed, we insert time, communication, and delay into the unfolding plot. We offer a needed re-set for all involved, just like we need in today's moments of uncertainty; a minute to think before we speak.

Responsibility Number Two: Master rapid analysis. To find and expand any conventional and unconventional resources, we train to alternative solutions. We get to know all potential scenarios before they occur; forecasting common trigger points, religious issues, addictions, what the latent passions create, and the most popular topics of hate. We are sensitive to anniversaries, known appointments on calendars, all available records, and social media. We interview anyone and everyone with information about those involved in the current crisis, threat, and owning historical data. We glean information leading to a small snapshot of those involved. Following a strict template, and relying on the full force of many minds, the blurry, partial image and inner life of the one-in-crisis appears. The forecast develops in minutes rather than days. We collect data quickly and make a judgment call based on incomplete information. The limitation of time naturally leads to an unfinished portrait; however, the partial picture continues to save lives.

Responsibility Number Three: Mine for enough data to save a life. The thumbnail view is enough to safeguard lives, a few pieces of a 1000-piece puzzle become essential to all facing threat and meeting the emergent need for helpful information. The Negotiator is a Mediator, just like you, creating magic with little information, and in little time. The template is set-up in advance, just like the process I'm encouraging for you. We create, double-check, and plan a strategy with no distractions.

Most situations last three to ten hours and the Hostage Negotiations Team mediates a successful outcome 95% of the time, and so can you. Offenders and the mess they've created get sequential order. We lure them away from their destructive thoughts and behavior and walk-through the crucial conversation without distractions. Most callouts are resolved with no further harm because we train to nearly every scenario before it happens, and so can you.

Actual crisis negotiations include a minimum of two trained negotiators, a primary and a secondary, and only one person does the talking. The secondary negotiator has a clearly defined purpose, to listen and watch for fatigue in the primary communicator. She or he listens intently to words, tone, volume, and is the only outside source communicating or offering suggestions to the lead negotiator. The secondary role, while rarely celebrated, is the most critical element; shielding the principle communicator from distraction. With full authority to relieve the principal negotiator at any time and for any reason, they can call for the interruption of services. The lead then transitions out of the negotiation and hands-off to a fresh communicator.

These details emphasize the reality of forecasting future needs for de-escalation and crucial discussion. Complicated conversations are only messy when negotiators break the rules and allow unconstrained distractions. Preparation and anticipation for a vital debate will minimize distractions in any crisis response, small or large.

Those who simplify the crisis usually solve the crisis, just like you.

QuikTip:

"Never rely on a prompt response by police. Assume the responsibility to de-escalate, flee, or fight."

Preventing harm is a goal attainable by anyone who has the desire, the basics of risk assessment, and the time to solve the problem. Naming the basic human need is simple. Assessing the probability of a safe resolution usually doable. Time is always a problem in our pursuit of preventing harm, and distraction creates the most significant challenge to time well-spent. Two final and relevant takeaways from the crisis negotiation experience include:

A. We start with honest intentions, and

B. While the scenario may end ugly, we believe in No Further Harm and in our ability to influence the positive change in others.

In most scenarios, you can make a safe judgment call with limited data; actions and preventative measures leading to 95% successful, non-injurious conclusions. Reducing damage, loss, and avoiding violence are possible without knowing the whole story.

Over-Analysis: A Fatal Distraction

Below a delay due to fear and procrastination, we find men and women frozen in analysis paralysis. Often challenging to recognize, delay and postponement seem innocent until we rush to complete what we have feared and delayed. Over-analysis only appears to be the problem, which is the constraint of time, limitations in the time left to solve a problem after the delay.

Over-analysis is popular, and the delay is rarely helpful in preventing avoidable harm and heartbreak. Waiting to take preventative action only after all the facts are known is a fatal flaw in many organizations and families. Postponing new policy, training, and delaying a crucial conversation with peers and loved ones equally hazardous. We find the innocent analysis mistake in nearly every threat that manifests to violence, school shooting, predictable construction accident, mass injury due to evacuation failure, airline maintenance flaws leading to mass fatality, and at every high-accident intersection. In far too many cases of predictable harm, we find someone, somewhere, and for some reason waiting for ALL the facts, rather than enough data to save a life. Forever considering possibilities before they act, implement, and before making the change happen, tragedy is nearly inevitable. It prematurely ends many careers in leadership.

Solution: Give Analysis a Deadline

Many organizations have successfully elevated the discussion around analysis, suggesting or defining the analysis threshold. CEO Bill Lewis and Bart Ricketts, joined by company Presidents Jeff Cleator and Gary Smith, have created a culture with healthy limits related to analysis. Lewis, a high-end 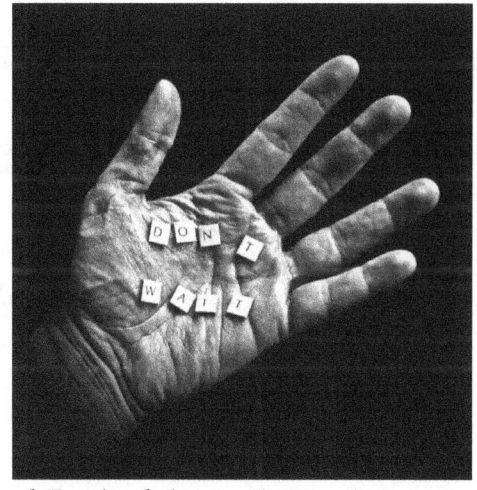 contractor, based in Seattle and Portland, has an impressive resume including Starbucks Corporate, Microsoft properties, and Boeing project management. Lease-Crutcher-Lewis promotes a belief that 80% is enough information to go ahead with a quality decision. The effective counsel works beautifully, supporting the need for knowledge, and informing employees they do not need to know it all. The conversation has filtered through the organization with ease and excellent results.

Leaders in highway transportation, where the speed of a threat (highway travel) is elevated, often promote 30% awareness for a healthy safety or engineering decision. Centers for Disease Control, responsible to contain potential epidemics, need less time as they work toward deadlines. Commercial Pilots need much less time. Speed is crucial when trying to analyze a sick or injured Jumbo Jet with 300 souls on board, and a rapid descent from 28,000 feet. Professional pilots may rely on the least data of all industries, 4-5% of the complete picture leading to action. Urgency teamed with courage and a checklist lead to a necessary and swift decision.

Each industry and every person respond differently; however, they recognize the threat found in delay, over analysis or distraction. We can easily apply the same attitude to our investment in the personal and professional analysis of our environment; long-term plans and urgent needs rest on a sliding scale. The need for rapid risk analysis without distraction is compared to the conversation needed or crisis before us. In the end, a mediocre analysis followed by a prompt decision will often save more lives than the perfect plan delayed by over-analysis.

Wildly different from most decisions made on and off the clock, forecasting harm typically demands a deliberate examination of our distant and recent habits and casualties. Assessing predictable and preventable losses call for the pursuit of all available information, while rarely incorporating a fully assembled puzzle before acting. The choices are usually made on the fly, using Good Faith, sidestepping distractions, and executing with little legal advice. Therefore, preparation is the mother of skill. Disturbances will present themselves in all scenarios, increasing vulnerability in many cases. Will you be prepared to engage, minus unreasonable delay?

"You will never do anything in this world without courage. It is the greatest quality of the mind next to honor."

-**Aristotle**

Chapter Conclusion

As I ask participants in formal training, what is your level of commitment to prompt change? If conflict creates delays or distraction, the solution is in a search for conflict resolution, the permanent solution over the avoidance underway. If the damage is of no concern, you're probably not the best person for tough decisions related to fear, procrastination, and other distractions. But if you seek the strength, tools, and the ability to forecast and can summon the courage to avoid the hazards of delay and diversion, you're on the right path and less-prone to over analysis.

The prediction and prevention of harm are flawed theories; however, the science, fueled by evolving knowledge, will morph quickly with your contribution. You can and probably will improve on the principles and values outlined in this chapter. Forecasting risk and sidestepping harm are open for improvement. I challenge you to enhance the process and pass it on.

End of Chapter Four

NOTES

CHAPTER FIVE

Assumptions: A Wakeup Call

It was a memorable moment, feeling trapped, and the only one in the audience of a seemingly small lecture hall, Trauma Room #3 of the Emergency Care Unit. It had been a series of mistakes, painful injuries, and a dash of unnecessary old-school shaming that prepared me for my future role as victim advocate. The informal critique was over, and the team of friends and co-workers had pointed out the obvious before leaving the room.

The Lead Nurse was the last to leave that night. She didn't continue the loop of reminding me not to reach into a running vehicle or the condemnation of the heroin-addict-became-violent-felon. She didn't harp on post-care, insurance coverage or medications. She leaned in and quietly told me, *"Every patient in this hospital has a story. Some don't share the lesson, and others never get the chance. Imagine the possibilities if every cardiac, cancer or trauma survivor shared what they have learned."* I don't remember her name but will never forget her light touch on my right forearm, gentle smile, and her courage in sharing those words.

...But I Knew the Rules

I had been in the business for about seven years, seemingly a risky period for skydivers, bull riders, and other industry veterans. I was a 27-year-old peace officer assigned to the inner-city of a sizable Washington community. I loved my job working the *swing shift* foot patrol downtown, a favored spot for courteous professionals, and after-hours drug use in the darkness and empty alleyways. I remember being intrigued by a transformation each evening. Those looking good, smelling good, and driving nice cars would slowly file out of the city. Shortly after dusk, and with those pesky pillars-of-the-community out of the way, the toxic night crew would file-in. Active addicts, alcoholics, and the Who's-Who of the desperate and hurting occupied the night.

The night I was injured was unusually dark, no moon, and a construction project required the temporary removal of street lights. I saw a man I knew as James, a late stage addict, seated in a parked truck. The blue, beat up rig; probably a nice Datsun pickup in its younger days, was dark and the motor was idling. Believing I knew James was flawed assumption number one. Eventually, an orange glow from a butane lighter reflected from his chest, chin, and face. James was cooking heroin and preparing to inject the drug. It was not unusual; I had experienced more than 700 low-risk interactions with nonviolent addicts each year, and this appeared to be more of the same. The thought process would be the second ugly assumption on my part. I noticed his small pickup truck was blocked in by a vehicle parked near or against the rear bumper of his subcompact. I assumed the large, unoccupied station wagon behind James would prevent him from driving. This move would prove to be life-changing assumption number three.

After approaching James and re-introducing myself, I reached in to turn off the ignition. Our life-changing decisions became dramatic, a poor choice by James and my tactical mistake lit the short-fuse. It would lead to a deadly chain-of-events, forever recorded in our history. I heard a loud and rapid acceleration of the engine and felt the vehicle move. With my hand and arm threaded thru a quickly turning steering wheel, we jolted rapidly in reverse, ramming and effortlessly moving the empty station wagon. I felt the pop and tearing of my joints, as my left shoulder, elbow, and fingers stretched to the point of dislocation. I could hear screaming, some of it my own, and the smell of burning clutch and tire rubber.

The life-threatening reality struck as we abruptly changed directions. Leaving the station wagon behind, we gained speed on the asphalt roadway; a frightened and desperate felon behind the wheel, and one injured, precariously perched peace officer hanging outside the driver's window. The entire interior of the small pickup was no longer dark, and images slowed for a frame-by-frame examination. I could see everything as if a bright light had been cast into the truck, supplying clarity and necessary details. The passenger had assumed joint-responsibility for driving the vehicle, and James, the driver, was focused on me. I was staggered to realize he wasn't trying to push me away or defend his drugs and his freedom. He was fully committed to hanging on to me until we reached the most destructive speed. It was no longer a mistake; this involved a team of two intending to kill me.

QuikTip:

"Unconventional times call for unconventional strategies."

The whys and wherefores I'll never know, but the stars aligned for me and not for James. I instinctively used my working hand to end the terror with deadly force. James released his grip, and I hit the asphalt with violent force, but a survivable speed. Part one of the ordeal, the longest six-seconds of my life, had come to a painful end for both of us. Regardless of what today's news and entertainment purports about the police, injuries hurt, and using deadly force is devastating. It was a horrible event, it was predictable, and I had missed the environmental cues and clues of danger.

Why?

While this is a police event, it follows the same pattern found in less dramatic cases. Like many injuries and fatalities observed daily in the lives of women and men in the workforce, traveling, and injured at home, this involved foreseeable risk, an unnecessary move by the employee (me), and the immediate results. Once again, we should consider the Five Dimensions of Predictable Harm:

The Environmental Norm: Conditions around James were far from ordinary; his behavior stood for a deviation from all-things-normal. My conditioning, the street-life of addicts and alcoholics and connecting daily, had fooled me, incrementally becoming my normal environment. Like any dangerous condition you may be exposed to regularly, I was forecasting based on my new norm.

External Clues: The external evidence of danger was present. Visible and clear clues were available but cloaked by a simple law called familiarity. I had become too comfortable around street-level addicts. Compassion, understanding, and empathy, while good traits in the real world, were not proper for the environment of street crime and addicts hurting for a fix.

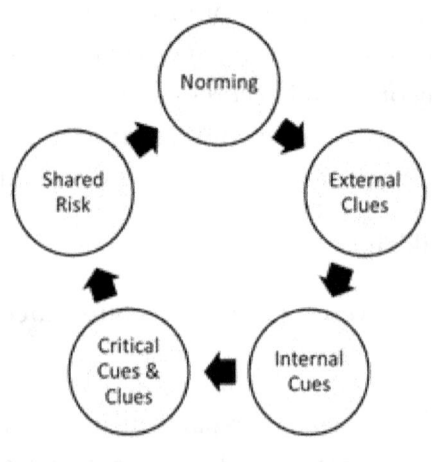

Even for the safety-minded, the inappropriate mental-state after long term exposure to an environment of moderate to high-risk is challenging to catch. Transit operators, construction workers, emergency room physicians, and nurses run the risk of the new norm. While we typically discuss the stress-response in terms of over-reaction, under-reaction is a reality in predictable harm. Awareness is key.

Internal Cues: While I recall a light gut reaction as I approached James, it was not enough to guide my physical actions to the desired 'all-stop.' Again, the insignificant adrenaline response contributed to the risk, constant exposure to potentially dangerous addicts had changed my thoughts, which numbed my natural reaction to danger.

In retrospect, I also believe I missed a clue known as Target Glance (described in chapter eight). Rewinding and replaying the incident in my minds-eye, multiple micro-flashes of his eyes likely supplied evidence. Several quick glances into his rearview mirror, sizing up the station wagon behind him with a uniformed officer inches away from his open driver's window, offered the deviation from the norm. His unusual attention to the empty station wagon would be considered unnecessary. James was likely measuring and weighing two potential threats to his freedom, a police officer and a station wagon. The abnormal glance (a zone-one clue, also defined in chapter eight) was a conceivable hint. Either way, I missed or did not consider the evidence. Yes, I still second-guess myself years later. Nothing to fear, the review is entirely natural in the world of PTSD recovery.

Stand-Alone Evidence: Stand-alone evidence or the clues and cues were present. This case involved not one but three red-flags; the vehicle engine was already running and a Stand-Alone Clue. The hypodermic needle, drug, and potential Bloodborne Pathogen was a weapon and a Critical Clue, and my somewhat hassle-free mindset offered a Stand-Alone Cue (low internal reaction was high-risk). While one stand-alone cue or clue is enough for an all-stop, pause, and re-evaluation, I continued to move toward the risk of harm; James, his full syringe, and his running vehicle.

Shared Risk (rapid communication): Dimension five includes the burden of what, when, and with whom should we share the vital message related to the risk. My patrol partner and I could have done a better job narrating and sharing observations during our approach to the truck used by James. Preventative communication is a stretch in this case. There was no shortage of rapid communication after the incident; affirming a safety policy and procedure already on the books. Bottom-line: The tactical error was mine, and mine alone; prompt communication did not take place or was thought unnecessary.

Please avoid locking-on to this as a police casualty, a distraction to those in a different role. This scenario, missing clues of danger, and the related harm happen daily in the form of accidents. This traumatic incident includes the theory aligned with my beliefs, pointing to clues of danger neutralized by my assumptions. Most mistakes go unnoticed. For others, the event or injury is never critiqued openly, leading to the endless and silent re-run of mental imagery and PTSD over many years.

The driver had committed a crime, but unlike the Costa Concordia fatality and Captain Schettino, James was not the solo-cause, and my lesson wasn't lost. The investigation did not end with James tagged as a solo-cause. There is rarely a single-cause or single-cure, and we should reject the conclusion when more information leads to the real lesson. I regretfully missed the clues of predictable harm. The five questions below, while not a formal assessment, clarify and re-introduce the template advanced in the introduction discussing Costa Concordia. Please consider the questions and make your assessment about the vehicular assault. In this assessment, like most, you may not have the information to answer all questions. A partial assessment is always better than no assessment. Good luck:

1. Was it predictable?

2. What was the distraction?

3. Does it call for conversation, intervention or penalty?

4. Is the cause trending?

5. What is the teachable resolution or short-term fix?

I had been trained and warned, NEVER reach into an occupied and running automobile. I had deviated from my training, lured by a near-fatal distraction in the form of assumptions. My internal response matched my false sense of security, and a response called "LO-LO" (lock-on, lock-out, a core-concept in chapter six). I locked on to my knowledge of the known driver, James, and locked-out the possibility he was dangerous. I locked-on to a belief the mass and weight were on my side, a one-ton station wagon is virtually impossible to move, and I locked-out the reality that I don't know jack about physics, mass, or the weight of a parked car. Finally, I locked-on to a flawed narrative; those who know me would never intentionally hurt me, and locked-out the fact, James is not the regular James. James is an addict desperately trying to get relief via the drug into his veins. He was therefore highly unpredictable. Tough lessons, indeed.

Naturally, that dreadful night left me with injuries, along with life-long gratitude and choices in how I handle the trauma. Surviving a brush with death after acting outside of my training opened my mind, and silent suffering has never been a choice. I'm not blaming the victim, myself, but acknowledging my role and reality of being linked to the chain-of-events. Predictable damage has a remedy, and the solution includes examining the part of the victim in the chain-of-events. We reduce risk by looking at every link of the chain. While acknowledging how the victim contributed may be uncomfortable, the move is crucial for constant and never-ending improvement; an honor to those forever changed before us.

Note: This case includes much more than I share in the book. I can discuss and write about this case because I went through hours of critique, critical-stress diffusing, and PTSD therapy. While I openly share all the details in the proper environment, this text is about avoiding the trauma rather than the many stages of treatment and recovery. If you, a peer, or a loved one is suffering after an incident or from combat-level distress, and symptoms exceed three-months, please get help. Treatment works and offers the freedom we all deserve. Much like predictable harm, PTSD includes various causes and cures. While on-line therapy rarely works, the web does offer great introductory websites. Options include BrainLine.org, legion.org, and cstsonline.org.

No Further Harm

No Further Harm, imitative of the famous oath coined by Greek Physician Hippocrates, was launched in the mind years before this text. *Primum non nocere*, which calls on us to *protect without creating a swathe of destruction in doing so*, would manifest while managing the police training academy. My interest began with historical research related to police officers, assaults, and fleet-vehicle accidents, eventually expanding to all preventable injuries. Predictable clues and cues went beyond intentional acts, high-speed pursuits, and policing. With the help of other organizations, I searched several careers and services to find and articulate the links in the chain of predictable harm. The examination included kitchen injuries to the 1986 ill-fated Space Shuttle. While I loved serving the public and enjoyed public safety, the examination of patterns, risks, and the victim-footprint was too limited.

Eventually, I organized a small focus group consisting of higher education, the medical and mental health community, private and public safety, and vocal activists from the city. I found their effort and cooperation amazing as we worked through a series of exercises. The group affirmed the short-term goals and agreed to the core concepts of predictable injury, accidents, and some criminal acts.

I traveled to fire stations, construction sites, football fields, and examined accidents within public utilities and services. I profiled accidental needle pricks in the emergency services environment, slip and falls in retail, predictable backing accidents and transit crime, school shootings, hate crimes, and the impacts of proximity to at-large, registered sex offenders. Most recent, I added the effects of mobile services, texting and driving, and how the phenomenon of e-completeness (full-time connectedness) elevates risk.

Once appointed to the Washington State Governor's Task Force on Trauma Care, I had access to facts and widespread beliefs. The role helped in naming other resources and possibilities as the prevention footprint continued to expand. I examined a lengthy list of frequent-flyers in the world of high accident intersections, childcare incidents, and victim-pilot profiles in airline fatalities. I also researched heroic saves. I weighed events involving experienced swimmers, rock climbers, and noncombat soldiers to the research. As you can imagine, the list had to be managed and restricted. I focused on the most impactful, the most vulnerable or operating without a beneficial risk profile, and those most at-risk and rarely assessed. I was intrigued by the common traits, human factors, and conditions leading to damage, loss, injury, and death.

I was also surprised by other patterns; a high number of casualties included predictable and preventable elements in more than working conditions. Behavior off the clock often presents a risky employee on the clock. Unresolved domestic violence, alcohol, drugs, and unscreened mental health issues may worsen in a typical working environment. The sequence leading to injury and death, often included off the clock behavior manifesting on the job. Examining the thoughts and attitude of the vulnerable party often lead to preventative measures. The evidence is clear and presentable; quantified and presented at home and in the training environment. The victim is still taboo; however, we can work around the curse with timing, tact, and diplomacy in our educational applications.

I would eventually attend and graduate from the FBI National Academy (session 211) in Quantico, Virginia. My instructors encouraged my studies, supplied stats, and shared highlights, best practices, and guidance. FBI Special Agents also shared inside knowledge and data that may help the public, schools, and the business community. They challenged my research, which was helpful. In the final stages of this project, we have a survival manual; Basics of No Further Harm.

The thesis has evolved, stalled, and morphed, eventually reaching beyond On-the-Job-Injuries to include something for everyone. The research challenges present-day myths with facts supporting the following:

1. Early intervention related to a seemingly minor observation is crucial; verbal warnings from others are often the only variable between injury and avoiding harm,

2. Forecasting and preventing harm is possible regardless of formal education, geographical residence, income or job title,

3. Tragedy usually needs a host; as much as we prefer to avoid the topic, a temporary victim mindset is part of the casualty equation,

4. Teaching predictable harm reduces, rather than increases fear,

5. Safety influence improves and erodes at every level; beyond a single-source or safety representative, practices maximized when all employees understand the five stages in forecasting harm, and

6. Once supported at the top, the safety culture can only survive if the masses choose to feed the safety culture with accurate data.

Words are not mandatory. Silent victims empower us with facts we may have missed in tragic cases. Re-examining old cases may lead

No Further Harm: A Purely Predictable Path

to the next generation of protection and lifesaving advice. The mistake, an injury, or the loss of a victim leads to new awareness, and it is a painful process for all involved. Without the close evaluation of the victim's role and relationship to the chain of events we skim the fringe and miss key facts. Those targeted by petty thieves, involved in an accident, or violated by global terror offer missed and predictable clues and internal cues. Not every time but much of the time, details within the vulnerable mind expose new tools, techniques, and a few secrets separating injury-free from the accident-prone.

Collective wisdom gives us the edge, as communication, humility, and care for our peers evolves within the framework of forecasting. We begin to capture the proper sense, a compilation of regrets, candid co-workers, and irrefutable evidence leading to a rare conversation. The positive culture of No Further Harm works quickly once endorsed at the highest elevation. Receiving the nod of approval from senior leaders is extremely helpful, but the change clicks with individuals at an operational level. Those at risk are ready for the discussion and already have skin in the game.

Safety is a personal decision with results reaching beyond the individual; a careful, factual and rational choice we make every day. From running a daycare, managing a home, to manufacturing fireworks, we can, and often do recognize, respond, and reconstruct our decisions based on predictable harm. It's time to look at the details and introduce a few unconventional signs and measures. Consider three tough questions, the same inquiry made in live training events:

1. If a human life relied on your assessment, would you read people, places, and things for a risk they may or may not represent?

2. When necessary, are you willing to consider, weigh, and share the presence of predictable danger?

3. Are you willing to recognize and suspend the Victim-Mindset;

acknowledging its role while revoking its dominance?

Answering these three questions offer a forecast; those dismissive of reading people, places, and conditions; unable to trust the gut or recognize a victim mindset may suggest this is not our time to work together. The proper prediction of harm is an uphill battle for those opposed to accepting the knowledge and responsibility to assess, evaluate, and share concerns. This crucial conversation, while never a comfortable chat, is my version of buyer-beware; 'yes' to the three questions paves the way for purely predictable ability.

We are exposing Risk for what he is; revealing the triggers and temptations for what he does and how he does it. As I've experienced in the past, you may honestly believe Risk shows up uninvited; a flighty and unpredictable animal we can tolerate like a drunk uncle, engaging as needed and by choice. By examining and discussing what victims have historically missed, we find a different version of risk. The risk is ever-present, recognized by some and lost by others; however, accidental injury and the regrettable fatality include specific ingredients. Those who predict harm know this and acknowledge a hazardous pattern quickly; the elements of danger begin to cluster. Those armed with knowledge often find the threat before the attack is fully prepared.

QuikTip:

"Threats change the expectation of privacy. Threats on social media should be taken seriously, treated like a live threat."

Anticipating harm is not new, but a package, supported by an operating system called attitude, loaded with facts about why some are safer than others. I've worked with investigators, insurance professionals, and safety experts who discuss the avoidable profile; however, they share the knowledge with alarming caution. Many have mentioned a blurry template of victimology, but resist sharing the truth in public. I agree it's never okay to share victimology or patterns in the presence of a grieving spouse, family or community. We postpone the discussion, delayed out of respect and packaged for future delivery. But the distribution of a life-saving message often never comes.

The lessons often fade with time; the teachable moment evaporates with the emotion, and the cycle continues. We move on from the injury or accident, regain confidence, and own a false sense of security. We throw the dice and re-enter a game of chance, minus specific lessons from the recent event. The false comfort, commonly called denial, becomes a gamble as the uneventful gap widens. In the end, we erroneously label individuals, neighborhoods, and entire communities as safe or dangerous without specific reasons why. We're about to discuss why.

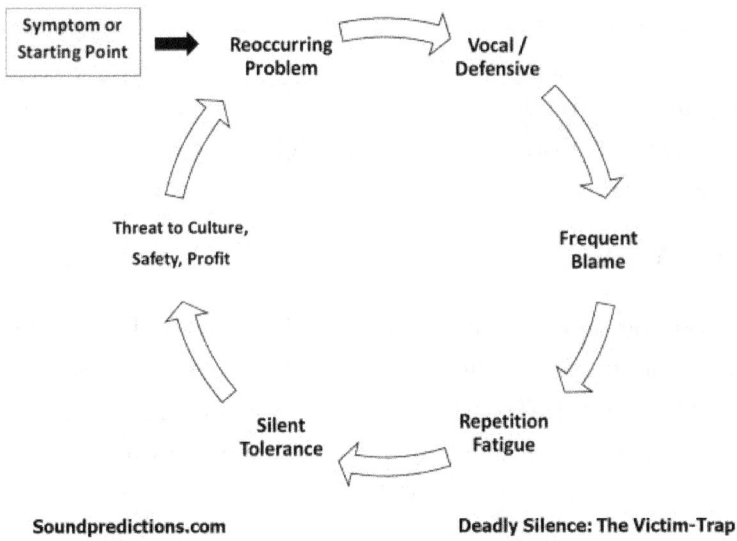

We've all perceived brilliant people using extraordinarily poor judgment; the lapse has forever-changed good women and men as it changed me. Those hit by a crisis are often in a dangerous albeit temporary mindset; common-sense seems to be on vacation. I've been the victim of my ignorance, my beliefs have adjusted. I am no longer surprised by a vastly different portrait of those financially ruined, injured, terminated from jobs, and occasionally killed. The contrary reputation includes those of above average intellect, reliable, stable thinking, with attitudes and behaviors worth modeling. There is no fixed-profile for a victim; however, vulnerability is measurable when considered with the changing and risky environment.

Figure 3: Illustration defined in Chapter Three, reoccurring conflicts, injury, ever-present danger; 'Fight & Forget' theory.

Digging deeper, I found many victims were off-the-beam at the time of their crisis. They were not in their right mind; thoughts, words, attitudes, and behaviors were out-of-tune and part of the temporary set-up for disaster. Victim-thinking is often a momentary lapse in awareness rather than a fulltime condition, and the victim condition has a cause and a cure. Answering why we drift in and out of the temporary victim-mindset is often the first and most crucial step in satisfying the need for resolution. The next step is equally exciting and urgent: We can teach others to avoid the process of victimization, a high-risk mindset, and high-risk employee behavior; forecasting harm is teachable.

Imperfect Works!

Preventing damage and loss can be exercised individually; however, the most significant multiplier of safety relies on the wisdom of the group. Together, we develop a system and a common language related to our assessment of risk. We can predict harmful behavior without a large volume of information. While accuracy is essential, the pursuit of 100% accuracy is a fatal fantasy, one I encourage each reader to avoid.

Our safety decisions need not involve irrefutable evidence; beyond a reasonable doubt is a legal standard rather than a life-sustaining process. I encourage safety decisions based on partial evidence known at the time; a small amount of useful information will often lead to the right conclusion - with a margin of error based on human biases and flaws. Yes! Bias and mistakes are part of the learning curve. The risk-reality prompts you and me to examine partial facts, think for a limited amount of time, and courageously act on the incomplete picture. Some say its Good Faith, and others call it intuition. It starts with changing how we judge rather than excusing our findings as a curse. The change may include training, which you can start right now! Those who improve how they judge their surroundings, master knowledge of their environment (norming) accelerate the speed and accuracy of their predictions. Know the norm, and you will recognize deviations from the standard (dimension number one in predictable harm).

Environmental Norming:

Environmental awareness is the foundation supporting our forecast, a sensibility right-sizing both atmosphere and risk. You already do it as an ongoing assessment of personal or professional routine. The norm includes the average condition related to safe-habits, standardized behaviors, and average conditions. The Norm is related to your day-to-day life; at home, work, exercise, recreation, worship, maintenance, housework, landscape, and child care. Norming only appears to be complicated, soaking-in anything and everything you consider part of your typical day and night. I suggest you relax and slowly begin to recognize the natural conditions in your home, work, and recreational life. Don't force the process; start noticing norms and deviations from the model.

Norms-of-Behavior, generated by long-term conditioning, often need intentional focus for a while. The eventual goal is to vocalize or describe why your observation includes a deviation from the conventional. Your behavior and that of each person, place or thing have a norm. The sound of machinery and cars, lighting, walking pace, the cadence of words, respiration, time of arrival and departure, and the tone of a meeting have a norm. Individual eye contact, weather-appropriate clothing, the sound of a voice, size of pupils, decorum, posters, bumper stickers, cleanliness of the individual, vehicle, workstation, and even that silly screensaver, provide the portrait of all-things-normal.

Prevention starts after we standardize our surroundings. The set-up allows us to notice a standard of living, cadence of speech, dress, or the safe and healthy condition. Once we master the norm, we recognize lifesaving changes in people, products, performance, positivity, engagement, volume, and levels of agitation. Forecasting is not reliant on the deviation because it differs from us, our preferences, or lofty academic standards. We notice because it is not the normal condition. Remember, we are not judging for legal, policy, or political reasons. A deviation from the norm calls for a closer look. The closer look saves lives.

Norming includes environmental standards and consists of the habits, cues, and clues present and practiced in our daily lives. We norm conditions each time we drive, recognizing and responding to deviations from the norm. Every warning light in your truck or car interrupts the standard. The sound of glass breaking and fenders crunching depart from the norm. Every chirp, beep, or tone is a deviation from the customary norm. A vehicle crossing the centerline is a deviation, a flat tire is a deviation, and unusual sounds from your engine are merely deviations from the norm. When driving, we rarely notice the normal behavior of other drivers but recognize variations from the norm.

In matters of medical health, it is the deviation from the norm that leads to recovery; every lump, bump, raspy voice, and irregular heartbeat supplies a warning. Changes in temperature, a flushed-face, a watering eye, and that throbbing tooth tell us something is off. We apply the same philosophy in our culture and atmosphere of safety. The norm changes before the slip, trip, or the active shooting.

No Further Harm: A Purely Predictable Path

Our internal awareness, active but often unnoticed before most tragedies, is equally impressive as it contributes to environmental norming. A gut reaction (Allostasis) is an internal mechanism we rarely discuss, which includes the process by which the body responds to threats and regains balance (Homeostasis). Stated differently, we have an environmental norm inside of us. Once aware, internal heat, coolness, a rush of nerve activity in the neck, scalp, and skin, offer a deviation from the norm. My experience, and the victim-experience provided by those interviewed for this text, often include the internal awareness or difference before injury, accident or assault (dimension number three in predictable harm).

If raised in the average home, it's quite likely your innate skills were the recipient of a dual diagnosis. Over the past 40-years, the western hemisphere has unintentionally promoted a cloud of suspicion about gut-level intuition. We know we must use judgment in creating and supporting safety; however, fear of reprisal and label often outweigh the obligation to notice a sensation, recognize, and share concerns. We often perceive a hazard and sense something is

wrong but sharing gut-level concerns is not supported by popular culture. Stopping a partner from taking a dangerous route may be popular in mountain climbing, but most would rather not comment when we believe policy may be hazardous, a person predatory, or on that unfortunate choice a peer is about to make. Historically speaking, split-second decisions are not today's problem; the best judgment call in high-stress situations is usually immediate. The foundation of No Further Harm promotes noticing more in our routines and communicating what we see more quickly. I believe in a philosophy that supports we may be wrong in our partial conclusions, but we share anyway. Share and apologize later but describe your concerns at once. Over-communication with positive intention is vital in reducing our risk.

The next chapter intends to exchange the awkward social silence for the opposite, which is over-communication. The group, not the individual, hold the popular wisdom needed for safety and application of a reasoned, fair, and broad approach. The problem is still in our common reaction, which is fear, silence, and a gamble that our internal response is probably incorrect. Worse yet we may trust our gut but fear the rejection or social media flogging if gut-level concerns are shared. The fatal equation is valid in nearly every case of mass violence and the active shooter. Someone, usually more than one person, had the gut-level reaction, noticed environmental clues and said nothing. Overreaction to warnings has not been a problem over the past 72-months. Caution, fear, and peer-acceptance are the present-day barriers to violence reduction and avoidable accidents. Not an opinion but a well-documented pattern of facts.

CHAPTER SIX

Core Concepts: Accelerating the Solution

Predicting harmful acts and assessing risk include the ability to forecast the outcome of some behaviors, a hazardous environment, and to consider worn or outdated tools before the tragic results hit home. Beyond general themes discussed in the first five sections, chapter six will narrow our learning path with mental models; instruments that discipline the mind, reduce distractions and accelerate the life-saving message.

Much like a favorite quote serving as the icon for a more significant lesson, we guide individual attention and focus using simple words as fuel for the memory. Our safety goals are often defeated when we continuously rely on compliance and policy when intuition and a gut-check is needed. Compliance is necessary; however, useless without the spirit of the law and speed in sharing the observation or evidence. Second to rapid communication, recognizing the ingredients of potential risk and danger is paramount. While some may believe the strategy is difficult to learn, it is far too important to ignore. The best personal and professional safety strategy includes the recognition of evolving patterns; the actual ingredients of the accident, criminal scheme, and incomplete formula potentially leading to disaster. The good news is you already do it;

you predict outcomes based on your history and a partial picture of the present threat. We are wired to forecast, destined to predict, and we often factor a calculated risk based on incomplete data or a partial view. Our pursuit of No Further Harm needs a few skills, learning the ingredients of danger, and lowering the threshold or trigger point for action. The balancing act is doable; ability is helpful while speed is crucial.

Like a Jigsaw Puzzle

Consider the developing imagery of a 1000-piece jigsaw puzzle. While the project is still incomplete, you are competent in understanding that a small, partial section of the mystery will lead to a grand image. The 1000-pieces may be a challenge until a small part develops and begins to make sense. You start with a single piece, avoiding the overwhelm found in the pile of 1000 confusing elements. You examine one clue at a time and begin constructing the majestic scene; eventually joining two pieces, then five, and finally, ten clues leading to a predictable pattern or the bigger picture. Like predictable violence or injury, you don't need the big picture to estimate the grand plan. Humans are fully capable, with a little training and practice, to know the outcome before the act, the injury, and before the mass violence.

The possibilities, based on a partial image, lead to more focus, energy, and decrease the need for the picture on the box. Within a fleeting period, we know the direction of our puzzle-portrait, and the process of completion accelerates. We can do the same in predicting and preventing harm; easily estimate our prospective risk. We can understand the image developing in front of us and enjoy an accelerated solution. We find the life-saving lesson in forecasting hazards, situations, and the rapid assessment of the not-so-nice human offender presented via the partial picture.

While the isolated puzzle experience isn't for me, some colleagues and friends find solitude in passing the time alone and assembling a jigsaw at their own pace. Some couples and small groups approach it differently; assembling the same puzzle using a team approach. They communicate, strategize, stop, and re-group. Verbalizing progress and tossing pieces across the table to others, they work on the corner, skyline, mountain, or the outside edge of the puzzle. The team is not distracted by the confusing pile of unassigned pieces; they focus on microelements that fit the context. Regardless of preference, the couple or small group completes the puzzle in record time. They use less energy, and by building on the collective wisdom generated by and through the group, they are more reliable. The individual may be proficient, but the group is more effective and rapid. Anticipating accidents and fatal acts follows the same line of thinking.

Our core-commitment to the reduction of accidental harm and intentional violence respects the wisdom found in the group. The individual can do it when needed and alone, but couples, families, and workgroups are empowered to do it better. When every person who can add to the solution does so, the risk is outnumbered, outclassed and often eliminated. Recent events illustrate we can't afford anyone passing time alone as they ponder all the pieces or clues of a possible threat. Recent losses in North America and Europe affirm the insanity of innocently withholding lifesaving information, trying to assemble all the elements of proof before sounding the alarm.

Finally, in promoting use of the group approach, if we can't weigh the risk before us, we have no warning to share. We scale and measure danger best as we discuss and share observations, clues and cues. My research plainly says without shared risk (dimension #5 of the forecast), the hazard multiplies, and injuries and fatalities increase significantly. It's more acceptable to deny the danger in silence; unable to define the partial picture, we close the window. A group rarely misses the pattern. This unstoppable team assemble the potentially tragic mystery in record time and prevent heartbreak.

Forecasting accidental injury and intentional harm, while more urgent than any jigsaw puzzle, includes assembling a partial picture of risk and danger. Often introduced in training, the strategic tools are refreshed by discussing and debriefing cases previously unknown to participants. Candid observations, regardless of opinions about forecasting, lead to nearly 100% accuracy in training scenarios. Nearly all adults and many children can forecast and understand how the trivial things contribute to a greater good or the big picture. We can predict based on the standard of No Further Harm, which is enough information, rather than proof, the popular approach and a failure.

The difference between needing proof and enough information to save a life, is in the precious time needed to respond to emerging threats. The proof theory is fear-based, leading to analysis paralysis, and a dreadful delay far too familiar. We'll never know if one-half of the fatal and preventable mass-shootings of 2017 were due to silence or a prolonged delay. We do know the well-meaning pause, waiting for a bright and complete image, has been named as a contributing factor in many cases of mass violence and catastrophic accidents in the recent past. People knew of the risk and said nothing. Many were waiting for the complete picture, all the data, and a case they could prove, rather than enough data to save a life.

A quick review of recent history supplies the evidence needed; predicting and preventing harm needs enough data to intervene, respond, or retreat and communicate. To wait, distracted by insecurity, the fear of being wrong, worried about being tagged as unfair, and self-centered concerns about image, contribute to the cultural barriers. Horrific casualties, disfiguring amputations, the death of children, and the premature mortality of beautiful people are linked to eroding communication. I've not been surprised by the reporting delay and ugly results, but the reason we stall and go silent is disturbing.

At the risk of repetition, we are suffering the consequences of competing values; preventable violence and injury need openness, while the fear of offending a fellow human stifles communication. The solution is near if we talk, train, and create a simple common-language. Optimum safety is the environment we're after and the priority; moving our efforts beyond the famous slogan of Safety First to *safety is our priority, even when it hurts feelings*. Our best practice includes sidestepping hypersensitivity, postponing petty conflicts, and allowing others the freedom to intuitively trust their natural ability to recognize danger before it has devastated a family, company, or the community.

QuikTip:

"Subtle-threat is an oxymoron. The offender should never remain at work or school after making a threat."

A partial solution includes reformatting the principals and values related to safety. The suggested change includes teaching and relying on the models most likely to produce rapid communication, minus the hypersensitivity. If not balanced and explained, the mixed message may lead to more silence. Silence leads to injury and death. Not an opinion but a 72-month fact-pattern.

Topic-Shift: Let's Talk Food!

Returning to the core conversation, training with the use of a simple cooking recipe often clarifies the lesson. Most training conversations around risk-reduction will improve with the cooking example. Humans recognize the goal of a chef before the meal is in the oven. In other words, the average adult and most children over eight years of age can construct meaning based on clues, historical reference, and context. I was recently honored to hear a flawless forecast by a brilliant 8-year-old. Her calculation predicted a family dinner nearly 24 hours before preparation.

After looking at an extensive list of grocery items posted on the refrigerator, she asked, "Mom, are we having meatloaf for dinner tomorrow?" Our young profiler had noticed four elements leading to her conclusion and question; lean hamburger and oatmeal were on the grocery list. A Pyrex cooking pan had been removed from the cupboard and placed on the stovetop. She also recognized the context or physical setting of her prediction. She accurately predicted the meal and the timeline based on four items or observations: Clue number one and two (oatmeal and hamburger) created suspicion, the tools (Pyrex cookware) staged for easy access, and the environment (kitchen) affirmed the context needed to make an estimation. With only eight years of worldly experience, she predicted the outcome (the meal) 24-hours before completion. The astute observation was correct, like lifesaving predictions of harm needed from our adult employees, teachers, and young students.

Clues, Context, Cues:

Clues and context lead to rapid and partial conclusions; ingredients and unusual behavior meeting the threshold as a deviation from the norm. In the case of predictable violence, clues and context may include increased absenteeism, a recent shut down of emotion, overly possessive of workspace and shared resources. Hints may be the detection of poor hygiene, consuming unusual quantities of alcohol, or new evidence of radical extremes. I've also measured ingredients consisting of unusual purchases or literature supporting a violent scheme, added to increased, unwarranted, and unassigned rage (no one knows the source, including him). The past and popular list has included a new obsession with darkness, celebrating or laughing at violence, and of course weapons.

I recommend policy and actions supporting the dignity of the group rather than the individual creating fear or concerns. This advice is 180-degrees from current practice in many cases. Respecting privacy when possible, healthy students, employees, and customers should become our priority as clues, context, and cues point to danger. When an employee or student has made a threat or become the subject of a pre-violence investigation, separating the individual from others is essential. The mass violence reported in 2017 included offenders who remained at school or work after becoming the subject of concern. Tact and diplomacy are important, but we can no longer allow the threat to remain with the likely victims. Again, we base our decision on recent history. The deadly recipe of clues, cues, and context, even if only a suspicion, calls for a quick conversation and action.

Not Convinced? Let's Talk Dessert!

Consider this scenario: While waiting for a friend, you notice a few items on the kitchen counter of his apartment. The evidence, listed below, might lead to an educated guess, a forecast, or a predictable act about to occur:

Cinnamon
Bag of flour
Bag of sugar
Bowl of sliced apples
Measuring spoons
Large mixing bowl
Round cooking containers

Some training participants believe apple crisp is in the future; others trust apple pie is the final product. If you guessed either, that's close enough! Congratulations. You just completed your first assessment and forecast! The dish is not complete, the oven is cold, and the Pyrex cookware is unused; however, your forecast was correct based on the evidence. Visible clues and context led to a conclusion based on experience. You considered, you judged, and you concluded. There is no dessert, no conversation, and only evidence someone is about to prepare a dish. Finally, by knowing the ingredients and recognizing the plan, you can prevent the final product. By removing one or more of the ingredients you interrupt the opportunity to fully prepare the dish. Accident reduction and violence prevention follows the same line of reasoning. We interrupt the act by removing one link in the chain. Without flour or sugar apple pie is not possible. Without a specific opportunity or victim condition, the act of harm is nearly impossible.

Ingredients of Possible Violence

Consider another dish about to be served: A co-worker has become unusually quiet over the past two weeks. While married, rumor has it he's staying at a local Extended Stay lodging facility. He has worn the same shirt for four days, he is unshaven, and his work boots are often unlaced, all abnormal considering his past. He was defensive when you tried to speak with him, and he reacted with anger as you moved his backpack from a chair you only hoped to sit. He snatched the backpack out of your hands saying, "Do I come to your workspace and snoop through your stuff?" He stormed out of the office with his backpack, mumbling something like "enough is enough."

After he left, you noticed a strange odor and several pieces of paper he dropped on his way out. The articles included a receipt showing he had recently bought toiletries, bleach, a roadmap, duct tape, and 200 rounds of firearm ammunition. Looking around his office space, you also notice all his framed photographs had been removed from the walls. What would you do? He has acted outside the norm but has not violated any policies, laws, or contracts. Officially speaking, he has done nothing wrong, and you have no legal obligation to act. Would you report your concerns confidentially? Quietly talk with others to further assess the risk? Or would you ignore it and toss the dice? Your call!

This case involved ingredients, context, and observable clues. With a few minor changes to respect confidentiality, these are the details from a case ending in workplace homicide and suicide. **Was it predictable? Preventable? Do you have an ethical obligation to act? Do you have a moral obligation to report?**

Ingredients of Predictable Accidents

In this training scenario you notice a co-worker appearing abnormally distracted, hypersensitive, and easily irritated. His uniform shirt is untucked, he's unusually quiet, and he didn't respond to your morning greeting. You later learn from the boss his child was recently diagnosed with Leukemia. The boss directs you to "give him space," saying "work is probably the best medicine. He doesn't want to talk about his kid."

Highly disorganized, the suffering co-worker continually forgets items needed for his job. He returns to the operations office four times before starting his shift, picking up another item needed for his task. Each time he runs back to the office his motorized equipment is left unlocked and running, a violation of policy. Thirty minutes into his shift you observe him talking on his mobile phone while operating the equipment, a public transit bus on one of the busiest routes. Mobile phones are also against the rules. You let it go. He needs his space. At 9:15 AM, three hours into his shift, the grieving and distracted operator struck and killed a cyclist. With a few minor changes to respect confidentiality, the scenario is gleaned from an actual transit accident. Let's apply the five questions advanced after the Costa Concordia incident. Your call:

1. **Was it predictable?**
2. **What was the distraction?**
3. **Does it call for conversation, intervention or penalty?**

4. Is the cause trending?
5. What is the teachable resolution or short-term fix?

The point is you can forecast the future, accurately predict outcomes, and rely on your human ability to judge. You CAN interrupt accidents and acts by recognizing unconventional elements and ingredients before the outcome. We must first notice the deviation from the norm by examining components (ingredients) potentially ending in accidents and violence. Then we communicate the risk (shared risk, dimension five), and it rarely includes "giving them extra space." In cases of accidental injury prevention ingredients (clues) may include fatigue, inadequate equipment, personal distractions, a hangover, a texting battle with a loved one, unresolved conflict with a peer, a flu virus, pending divorce, another mobile call, and recent mistakes. All deviations from the norm.

We watch for patterns, ingredients, and deviations from the norm. If we recognize the elements or behaviors threatening safety, we have an excellent chance to predict and prevent harm before the act. We call this forecasting; understanding the environmental markers, speech, and other norms; allowing you to recognize the deviations from the standard. Eventually and naturally, we accelerate our ability to forecast with time; the ingredients line up and cluster quickly. The early forecast and common-sense preparation minimize the damage. Violence, intentional slow-downs, sabotage, harassment, destruction of brand and morale, and harm to all relationships, may be avoided by respecting the five essentials of forecasting.

Refresher: The Five Dimensions of Predictable Harm:

1. **NORMING**: Identification and understanding a stable norm or safe environment,

2. **EXTERNAL CLUES:** Useful or unusual evidence of danger; words, equipment, external signals, and potential clues that deviate from the norm,

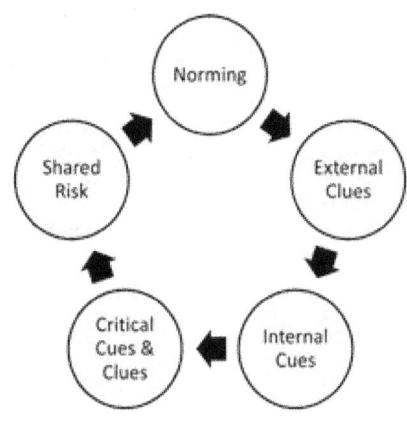

3. **INTERNAL CUES:** Internal warning signs that depart from your standard feelings of wellness and safety. The internal cues include the not so popular gut-check, the internal-atmosphere many have learned to ignore, and our natural intuition drowning in distractions,

4. **SOLO OR STAND-ALONE EVIDENCE:** A single warning sign (clue) or internal reaction (cue) making no other evidence necessary. A solo and undeniable threat; weapons, violent conditions, etc., and

5. **SHARED RISK** (rapid communication): The need for and acting on a rapid communication strategy. Knowing with whom, when, and why our immediate communication is necessary.

With practice, forecasting risk will become automatic and intuitive. Eventually, students can describe simple elements and a decision to take no action or crucial ingredients of extreme danger needing immediate attention. The goal includes making this a natural part of daily observations minus the adrenaline-dump. Over a lifetime or career, your views and keen ability to forecast will likely lead to the ultimate prediction. Recognition of the partial image will save a co-worker's life, the life of a loved one, or prevent a career and life-threatening disaster.

Most patterns, a few meaningful pieces of the puzzle, are low-key and unspectacular, some scale as dramatic. The practice of forecasting stays constant and fundamental. Your assessment may lead to awareness and a minor course-correction, or the ingredients may add up to a fatal concoction we act on at once. Urgency may shift to dynamic, but the daily habits and process usually remain static. Those who become the best in this practice apply the skills every day, research or discuss the topic weekly, and include a partner in their effort.

The rest of chapter six includes supporting concepts, attitudes, and suggestions to lower the risk of accidental and intentional harm. These are the icons and quotes I rely on as I scan my surroundings for danger. While I never expect full acceptance by a student or reader, I encourage choosing of three or four fitting the need found in your environment:

Concept #1:

Every Human Act Includes Opportunity and Desire.

Concept one is the foundation of prevention whether we are discussing an assault, road rage, a bully, a shop-lifter or a global terrorist. The risk of harm drops once the offender loses his desire or his opportunity. Most people try to target desire; however, the reality states we have little control over desires fueled by rage. Those who harm burn with strong passions. I advocate a focus on opportunity reduction. One can easily see why risk and prevention do not focus on the complex desires and motives of a rage-based heart, as this is a science of its own. If we stay focused on opportunity, desire often becomes irrelevant.

Concept #2:

The Act Of Harm Happens Twice; Once In [The] Mind, And Again Upon Execution Of The Act.

Intentional Harm: While it may be rapid, those who intend to harm us must plan, process, and gather all the tools (mental and physical) to process an attack from thought to action. This process rarely involves a refined plan or conspiracy. The process leading to harm, a gap between ideas and action, will last seconds, minutes, or hours, and the gap makes harm predictable and therefore preventable.

Accidental Harm: The absence of a plan, dismissing the risk, preoccupation or distraction is first, and the cue happens in the educated mind. Loss of focus is first, and the injury or near-miss follow. Accidental harm occurs twice; loss of awareness, which makes it predictable, followed by damage if we miss the cue of preoccupation. While some exceptions exist, concept number two is usually present in cases of preventable accidents.

Intentional and accidental harm usually involve signals, clues, cues, words, and behaviors that present the opportunity for prevention. Once trained or allowed in the case of employees or students, potential victims, witnesses, and support staff will notice a departure from standard practice; recognize the patterns in predictable harm before the act.

Concept #3

Understand The Cloak Of Secrecy.

While Hollywood highlights visible crime and drama, this is only an illusion. We believe the criminal act, the actual assault, sex offense, or event, account for less than three per-cent of the overall scheme. In other words, 97 percent of the offender's time goes into planning, the collection of information, watching, stalking, online activity, and selecting the scene of his future crime. Stated differently, he is trying to bolster confidence and prefers to plan in privacy and secrecy, as anything else would endanger his bizarre mission.

Fortunately, the offender is often sloppy or undisciplined in his clandestine mannerisms. Without noticing his flawed approach, he exposes plans with his collections, purchases, not-so-subtle leering, social media messaging, unwanted contacts, surprises, and words that deviate from the norm. His attempts at secrecy are often visible. Once we understand the need for secrecy, we will notice their effort. An innocent interruption, inquiry, or challenging their secret will usually confirm our suspicion and heightened risk. A subtle approach may be necessary, only tried with the proper support. In most cases, the reaction is helpful, lowering concerns or confirming a need for follow-up. Never confront unless prepared for the adverse reaction.

Concept #4

Forced-Teaming Awareness.

Forced teaming is a verbal, written or behavioral control tactic used by the offender; a form of pressure or manipulation by phone, social media or face to face. The conversation may include the unusual use of *We, Us, Our time, We wouldn't want that, would we? Our plan, We believe, We think, and Our future.* Usually creepy the first time we hear it, this is an attempt to imply a relationship that doesn't exist. Once aware of this dirty little trick, it is easy to catch.

Beyond words, forced-teaming is a tactic. It may include the impromptu meeting in a grocery store, on a jogging path, or on the sidewalk near a work assignment. . If the offender is using this approach, he is trying to close the gap between he and a future victim or current witness. He may sign up for local volunteer positions, clothe himself with a new brand, alter travel, develop a fictitious need leading to your services, triangulate with a friend to close the distance, and get a vendor position, just so he can *team-up* with you. Please remember, teaming language is also used innocently; popular among teachers, nurses, and other caring people. Teaming words are a positive tool. Forced-teaming is not. We should consider the context. Plus, this one rarely stands alone. I have not crafted a forecast of potential harm solely based on forced-teaming.

Concept #5

Energy Follows Thought.

Concept #5 further clarifies the predictability of destructive and harmful thinking, the curse of unmanaged thoughts. What we often ponder leads to our acts. There are many approaches in recognizing what takes place in the mind of the offender. His behavioral clues act as indicators and warnings, alerting you to the thoughts, plans and actions. Any offender must collect information, make inquiries, and may ask questions vital to him, but unusual to the rest of us.

Healthy people freely expose their thoughts, evidence supports positive attraction, hobbies, and vices. My friend is an avid windsurfer and the evidence is everywhere. Books and magazines, conference brochures, posters, bumper stickers and even some jewelry will tell you about his passion for windsurfing. Words are not needed. What my friend reads, collects, and on-line research expose his thought-life before any utterance. And that's exactly what our bad guys do, to the negative.

Most important, the thought-life is in-play before deviant behavior (energy resulting from continuous thinking). A long list of clues illustrates his inner thoughts. Thoughts also show up in the quiet collections made by the offender. Books, magazines, posters and bumper stickers supply a hint. Coffee mug logos, to-do lists, framed photos, incoming mail, and memberships expose his thought-life. We can recognize dog lovers by their clues and collections, passionate golfers by what they read and watch, and wine connoisseurs by how they swirl, examine and smell a glass of wine. No words are necessary. The same applies to those with a passion for harming others.

Often fantasy based, the offender mentally rehearses his act hundreds of times to lower anxiety. His confrontation with you intends to be a low-stress interaction, as pondered in his immature mind. His delusional plan often includes no resistance. He rarely considers any possible interruption to the sequence of events threaded through his active fantasy. Upon execution, the reaction of surprised victims is contrary to his mental scheme, and violence may erupt.

Strange as it is, the offenders intentions seem to reach the victim's subconscious mind first, creating unexplained anxiety (dimension number three, internal cue). Many interviewed for this text experienced a lump in the throat, a churning in the stomach, or a mild rush of heat or coolness in the face, chest or scalp. Don't minimize internal cues because you can't explain the cause. Pay attention to these reactions, create space first, and protect yourself. You're not going crazy but may be in danger. You should walk away, leave the table, ask a third party to remain with you, or skip the elevator rather than enter. If on a sidewalk, consider going to a home, flagging down a car, asking a stranger to stand with you for a moment, or step off the curb and scream for help. Potential offenders hate it when their plan is not going well. Bad guys will often flee in response to the reaction. If he's an innocent good guy, he'll likely stand there with a surprised look. If you're wrong, you are alive and can apologize later. Screaming has never killed anyone but failure to yell certainly has.

Concept #6

LO-LO: Lock-On, Lock-Out:

Affecting our vulnerability to accidental or intentional harm, LO-LO affirms our need to remain flexible and open to changes in what may lead to a casualty. If a pilot assumes her highly polished plane does not need a detailed pre-flight equipment evaluation, the assessment may be flawed or not done at all. She locks-on to the reliability of the equipment and the spectacular safety record, locks-on to only the facts supporting her positive bias, and locks-out the need for a complete pre-flight assessment.

The LO-LO infraction is in our shortcuts, and the long-term or incremental erosion of safe practices. Examples include blind belief in untested safety equipment, avoidance of pre-checks, and the speed thru an unmarked and familiar intersection. LO-LO is in-play by trusting a climbing harness is just as safe this year, that a low crime area is still low, and the ice on that favorite ice-skating pond is just as safe as last week. We might lock-on to the lethal lie telling us the air quality in a confined space has not changed since our last check, and that sweet guy who greets you on your running trail every morning will remain sweet.

History says we believe risks resolved in the past remain resolved; we lock-on to the belief those hazards addressed last month remain safe. We may lock-on to a conclusion the danger has not changed; however, the risk is best recognized by considering all-things-new. Any gap in time, a new relationship, or frequent use of equipment calls for renewed scrutiny. New employees make it fresh, old equipment regenerates risk, and hundreds of environmental changes refresh the need to respect the reality of LO-LO. Remember, assumptions lockout sound practices.

Concept #7:

Know Thyself First.

This concept is vital in avoiding accidental or intentional harm. Only one person has the information about fatigue, muscle strains, a virus, preoccupation, underlying anger toward the coworker, and frustration over daily stressors. Only you understand the vulnerability exposed on that day, hour, or the moment when harm decides to strike. And only you know when you shouldn't be interrupted. Those dedicated to safety must be committed to self-awareness; awareness of one's weaknesses, and fully conscious of harsh biases. To know the threat, we must understand how we tick as individuals.

I treat human and accidental risk as an ever-present force calling for calm awareness over paranoia. Danger floats by undetected; drifting quietly through each car, machine shop, truck, job site, flight deck, daily commute, vacation home, shooting range, and every surgical ward. He is odorless and tasteless as he examines all opportunities to strike in secrecy. Searching for the soft spot, Danger will pause and carefully examine your weak spots; evaluating and measuring deviant opportunities, he decides to hit or move on. Danger will give you a pass or use your weaknesses against you. He does this with surprising speed and accuracy, preying on those who do not know themselves. And when you understand what Danger knows, Danger often moves on, frustrated by self-awareness.

Knowing ourselves is unconventional, healthy and life sustaining. Understanding the condition of our body, our reactions, standard errors in judgment, and current distractions. Awareness of enhanced risk when suffering illnesses, a recent death in the family, and knowing all current liabilities will reduce both accidental and intentional risk-of-harm. A solid self-check before we step into our day or night, and more often during stressful times, pay big in the long run. Enhanced safety is in the details; how hunger impacts judgment, lack of water leads to lethargy, the impacts of medicine we've started, or the caution needed as we stop prescriptions or a relationship. The Danger is forever frustrated by individuals and teams that practice self-awareness. When we can see ourselves, understand our circle of influence, and right-size our ego, risk drops and morale ticks upward. Finally, to know yourself is to know when you're in over your head and when outside resources may be necessary. Know Thyself First promotes the humility to ask for help and outside opinions.

Concept #8:

Unconventional Times Call for Unconventional Strategies.

As I mentioned earlier, we can lower risk, but we can't end it. Added effort and continuous learning are critical. To thwart and frustrate persistent threats, we stay flexible, aware, and fully prepared for the unconventional change in style or a different scheme. There are only a few constants in the criminal mind and the scenario of harm; however, a shift in style is inevitable, and offenders adjust to our improvements. Accidents have more variables than the intentional act. By staying vigilant, applying these concepts to our daily walk, and supporting an open mind, we slide from denial to enjoy a well-earned part of hope. Unconventional times are those periods during travel, on a new job site for the first time, and moving to a new area. As beautiful as it may seem, new is unconventional. New calls for caution; in a new place, the new boss, the equipment, the vehicle, the fresh exotic meal, the hobby, the sport, and even the new dog call for unconventional scrutiny, alternative care, unconventional patience, focus, and listening.

Concept #9:

Constants Aren't.

We can lower our risk by understanding formulas, laws of nature, and the power of a good plan, but blind trust in knowledge alone is a big mistake. A brilliant man with NASA shared concept nine. During our conversation about the Shuttle Missions, he described dazzling calculations by the ground crew, flawless execution by the astronauts, and the construction and launch of a vehicle consisting of literally 2.5 million parts. When examined individually, product, propulsion, and mathematical equations are constant. Once combined for a mission, the mix is anything but continuous or reliable. Mr. X described NASA employees as dreamers; hundreds of people who made the dream take flight, followed by hectic problem solving to keep the dream from crashing. Engineers, pilots, astronauts, and physicists became master problem solvers, and that's what they do for every mission. To prepare for each launch, he explained, they agreed on one thing; Constants Aren't! The resulting humility and open minds led to many successful NASA Shuttle Missions.

Concept #10:

Unspoken Expectations are Pre-planned Conflicts:

Most adults understand the importance of communication but might not grasp how stress has a chilling impact on getting the words out. We connect and reduce harm by communicating; however, we influence change by describing how to lower risk in the short-term. Clear expectations often lead to overcoming barriers to safety more quickly as problems arise. When I do not get the  response I hoped for, I often find I was unable to describe clear expectations or simply forgot. You can be confident in your message by defining the expectation, knowing the reason behind expectancy, and the goals you hope to meet. I prefer to seal-the-deal by describing the first step toward the goal and having that first step repeated back to me.

Concept #11:

Get Cool with Conflict:

Safety and security significantly improve with succinct language and clear boundary lines. Statistically speaking, risk increases for those who suffer from weak or nonexistent property lines. Asking for what we need, require, and respect comes to those with confidence. Confidence comes to those who are cool with conflict. Getting cool with conflict doesn't encourage or call for battle. Concept eleven states we don't avoid conflict because it creates discomfort. When communication fades or becomes non-existent, when we avoid the conversation needed to prevent workplace violence or accidents, fear of conflict is often the cause.

Concept #12:

Don't Insist on Proof When You Have Enough Information to Prevent Harm:

Many academics and some safety experts rely on legal thresholds in estimating risk; before issuing a warning, they must have all the data. The fallacy in needing a complete portrait of danger before warning others is a fatal flaw! Following the examples supplied earlier and found in the picture of the active shooter shared later in the text, the incomplete puzzle or a partial list of telling ingredients pointing to harm, should be enough. Issue a warning or start the private discussion first, and then confirm with facts. This is the cultural change recommended by recent history; a crucial conversation needing less information, and more courage without the condemnation.

End of Chapter Six

M.K. Mann

SoundPredictions.com

NOTES:

Confidential On-line Assessment

MyRiskChecklist.com

CHAPTER SEVEN

Physical Surroundings & Safety

Chapter seven presents helpful tips often overlooked in the physical environment. Our discussion will include avoiding the victim-trap as we vacation, settle into a new office building, and size-up any structure, hotel, or the real estate environment for the first time. We'll also discuss opportunities missed and evaluate our current circumstances with fresh eyes and a new strategy.

Like others enjoying a busy life, a meaningful assessment often becomes a chore for the safe and comfortable. The problematic reality includes high-risk in both the familiar and not-so-familiar world. Optimum safety calls for full-time awareness, accepting the safe routines of yesterday may consist of new danger by the introduction of a new hazard or threat. The most familiar environment, the route or parking area traversed daily may have become not-so-familiar after all.

Refreshing the assessment of risk is necessary and unpopular; respecting new conditions with each new employee, weather, new neighbors, new structures and those affecting lighting conditions or visibility, new or worn equipment, and surprises created in a rapidly changing world. In cases of intentional harm, many variables may lower or heighten risk. A simple change, such as traffic detours place us in a new neighborhood, exposed to changing criminal styles.

New risk goes beyond new neighbors. We should enjoy our old neighborhoods; however, I suggest we avoid falling in love with our old awareness. We may not catch subtle changes and not-so-delicate additions, such as a new danger in traffic and construction projects or the half-way house for newly released sex offenders. Our existing job sites may become relaxing, even though we have a new generation of thieves, saboteurs, corporate hackers, and eco-terrorists. Also, if we believe our environment has not changed, we must consider changes to our hearing, reaction time, safety biases, temporary illness or a new preoccupation clouding our thoughts.

When it comes to alien territory, we stay guarded for about 28 days. Following a natural decline in vigilance, we often embrace blind trust in all-things-seemingly-routine after 90 days. We return to the static life, tempted by old data, predictable routines, easy shortcuts, and often do so confidently and without challenge. The use of old data in a world of new hazards is usually a set-up for serious harm. Once you become too comfortable in any existing environment, the risk will tick upward until we slow down, examine the territory, noticed new risks and set up a new norm. Awareness is the first step.

The Myth of Experience

A new employee introduced to an unusual or different worksite will generally experience a thorough orientation, which includes a series of cautionary notes. I found virtually no increase in risk or harm for a new employee under the watchful eye of a trainer, journeyman or when following a structured orientation. The new revelation tells us risk escalates rapidly when seasoned employees begin work at a new job site. Experienced employees without the alignment of old knowledge and new hazards, suffer greater risk and casualties. New equates to inexperience; any employee swimming in new danger and those with years of experience should be considered a green employee for a limited period. Seasoned workers ramp-up

No Further Harm: A Purely Predictable Path

quickly, however, their risk of harm is elevated as they begin a new role or transition to a new location. The general rule, often described in my circle as Green-Risk or Green-Harm, holds true off and on the clock.

I found the myth-of-experience in many cases, risk creeping up side-by-side years of experience or age. The level of comfort in work task, a new community, vacation destinations, a new nightclub or a new jogging path. Once beyond the first experience, the minute the honeymoon with awareness has passed, and after a series of injury-free days, our safety deteriorates. The new community grows familiar, and we respond with another screening for hazards. The common vacation destination should be re-considered for risk, that usual gym or nightclub may have a new danger, and the trusted jogging path scrutinized as not-so-trustworthy. Recycling our assessment is difficult, but it pays big when risk is exposed and avoided.

We find solutions in a deliberate decision to focus and respect global rules of safety; formulating our first forecast of risk relies less on personal knowledge, shifting to the international recipe for safe practices. Predicting and preventing harm in unfamiliar or familiar digs is still doable as each environment speaks to us; announcing both strengths and vulnerabilities via external clues of risk. Every property, each home, and all job sites project an image; words are helpful but not necessary as environmental clues tag the location as seemingly safe or desperately dangerous. The challenge in green conditions will need a measure of commonsense, focusing on physical property first.

Chapter seven will focus on new job sites, properties, vacation sites, and buildings, with a dash of risk-reduction via environmental design. The landscape, lighting, litter, and even upkeep and TLC support our lifesaving forecast. Conditions usually project vulnerability long before residents, pedestrians, and customers.

Refreshing the forecast is not a novel idea, but a lesson-learned from those who previously did not forecast heightened risk in familiar territory. We lower vulnerability by slowing down, understanding our status as new-on-the-block, and reminding ourselves 'constants aren't.' The flawless hiking trail trudged last year is not trustworthy until tested today. Last year's best practice may not be best this year, and that simple re-inspection of a sturdy structure should not be considered routine. According to statistical data provided by OSHA and the FBI, casualties in an unfamiliar environment are preventable. We avoid blind trust by relying on a current forecast; testing assumptions, inspecting safety equipment, and confirming practices.

I suggest we soak in an unfamiliar environment like those learning a new topic in school. We slow the pace, dedicating more time and attention to detail. Refreshing core concepts will place you in the top 5% of those least likely to become a victim. Some of our skills and a part of our past assessments always apply; however, not all hazards or lessons from our history fit in new surroundings. Many pay the ultimate price every year; falsely assuming the world is a cluster of consistent conditions. We should always challenge the assumption; questioning, confirming, and communicating our challenge will become the standard of care in a genuine culture of safety. Through determination, humility, and extra time the realities of risk come into focus, and we are free to enjoy another day.

Myth: Risk & Time of Day:

Many have suffered casualties over the past 72 months entertaining a belief that Risk is a day sleeper, resting like a vampire and stalking victims in darkness. Once again, contrary to the Hollywood indoctrination, individual risk spikes in the brightly lit environment. Because the light of day might fool us, an extra measure of awareness is needed. We should refresh our perspective by remembering accidents are a 24-hour affair, increase during daylight hours and trend-upward into the evening hours. We often drop our guard during the day, and while most drunken driving incidents occur at night, the volume of all other vehicle accidents occurs between 3 and 9 P.M.

Serious misconceptions exist on-the-clock; not shocking, but a few 2018 conclusions might surprise you. The untimely death on the job will likely occur after a restful weekend, striking on a Monday or the first day of the work week. More specifically, harm sneaks up on us within the first two to four hours of the first shift worked. Bottom line: low awareness throughout the day is a fatal flaw, and fair-weather casualties lead the pack in the USA, Canada, and Europe.

Universal Guidelines: Environmental Hazards

Those who plan or inflict intentional harm select a scene environment based on measurable but straightforward observations; our career-crook is obsessed with the risk of exposure or capture. The offender rarely understands why he selects one location over another; he scans the landscape looking for low-risk opportunities, which happen to be our high-risk properties. The criminal rarely enjoys a solid plan as he picks his next scene. He's initially cautious but suffers consistently from a lack of focus; his behavior is reckless, selfish, and usually aggravated by addiction, or made while under the influence of both drugs and alcohol. I highlight this mental state for two reasons:

1. The offender is dangerous but predictable, and

2. We can distract and detour the offender; safeguards are possible as we strengthen the risk-presence of potential victims and the visual profile of the workplace or property.

The offender is rather shallow, often relying on the imagery rather than facts. Bad guys usually begin the end of a poor career choice when they select a well-prepared victim suffering from poor optics, only appearing vulnerable. On the contrary, people and properties that look well-fortified often get a pass from the offender, even when the area is susceptible underneath the veneer of seeming secure.

Offenders Search for Criminal Curb Appeal

I've spent thousands of hours studying the unnamed offender and twice the time on the environment he prefers; his choice and scheme become our playbook in prevention. In cases of the unknown relationship, anonymous offenders prefer a cloak of secrecy in broad daylight; freedom to scout properties without exposure is their priority. The need for an undetected mission and deviant search limits includes a cursory view of the next potential victim-premise. His choice is almost always a foggy mental snapshot with the perfect criminal-curb-appeal. The atmosphere, with or without people, draws his attention. The good news: while we don't know his name, we do know what he's looking for, why he selects his target, and why he avoids other properties. This knowledge has a compelling purpose; once shared and respected, the details elevate our safety.

Targets, statements, victim portrait, style, behavior, obsessions, and a trigger point for rage are impressive; however, the physical conditions and the location supply lifesaving information.

Optics Reduce Accidents & Intentional Acts

Finally, the environment considered high-risk for crime is like many pre-incident conditions of an accident or the scene of an innocent injury. Often unkempt, repeat accident and crime scenes are often disorganized, appear neglected, include trip-risks, poor lighting, expired fire extinguishers, used first-aid kits, emergency eye-wash stations gone-dry, inspection certificates missing, and have not been kept or cleaned. Nasty things often happen in an ugly and neglected environment.

This chapter will define thirty-plus dimensions of a safe physical environment, an effective tool to lower vulnerability. I suggest examining the definitions below from two perspectives:

1. **The environmental clues warning you that the area is potentially unsafe, and**

2. **Reliable advice for those interested in enlarging the cosmetic and physical safety footprint.**

Remember: The environment speaks on its own; while some of my clients love to post signs and grave warnings, the property projects a message long before human communication or signage.

Four Pillars Supporting Your Environment

The foundation of a safe environment begins with four props; a philosophy built around a core set of principles based on the belief that effective use of design can lead to a reduction in the risk of harm. While the offender has a psychological profile, our surroundings have an environmental projection. Beyond conventional safeguards, we rely on natural forms of surveillance, access restraint and territorial support for positively shaping the perspective leading to safe human behavior. It is through these theories dating back centuries, my clients, students, and you can intentionally develop the environment with simple changes and low-cost support. We can also view all environments differently, and recognize the nasty spots disrespecting visual laws, and therefore sidestepping uncertain environments.

Consider the possibilities as we select when and where lighting, landscape, open spaces, and human activity can help safety increase profitability and, through this process, lower our vulnerability. Intelligent use of space can also minimize conflict and ambiguity with a rational plan. While we only introduce the four pillars of preventative design in this text, many resources, including myself are eager to supply added guidance. The definition and design of our space prove useful in reducing risk; intended activity areas are high function while increasing a sense of wellness, security, and encouraging ongoing partnerships, all at a low cost. The four pillars include:

Pillar #1, Natural Surveillance:

Opening the line of sight when possible is the spirit of natural surveillance, privacy but allowing our property an unobstructed view 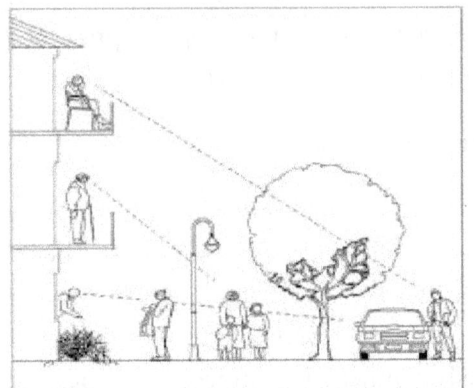 from within the property as occupants look outward. Risk and vulnerability drop, crime is reduced, and the atmosphere improves as we open the natural surveillance. It starts with landscape and lighting with an emphasis on opening the line of sight rather than blocking visual clues and enclosing property with plant growth and walls.

Pillar #2, Natural Access Control:

Natural Access Control is the opposite of fortification, beyond a coil of military razor wire, electric spotlights, or the eight-foot fence adorned with spikes. These are examples of humanmade access control; obvious, clunky, and less-friendly. Natural Access Control is subtle, attractive, and lures people in for all the right reasons. Clear pathways guide, beautiful fences suggest, lighting encourages, and landscape supports the intended user. Without a word whispered, pure motives are comforted while deviant intentions shy from natural access controls, to guide people and vehicles to and from the proper entrances. The goal of physical access control goes beyond spot-checking intruders, to serve in decreasing the opportunity for crime by inviting wanted customers and intended users.

Pillar #3, Territorial Ownership:

Territorial ownership is the principle that encourages absolute claim. This belief favors the impression of the undeniable territorial claim; the image projected but received differently by intended and deviant users. We can design  and highlight the line of influence with suggestive lighting, pavement treatments, landscaping, helpful signage and colors that develop a sense of proprietorship. Territorial areas clearly distinguish themselves from private. Potential trespassers perceive this area off-limits and intended users or guests guided to the proper entrance or meeting area.

Pillar #4, Maintenance & Preservation:

Landscape, clean lines, and lighting send a message, and it is a two-part signal; if supported, they suggest care and responsibility. On the other hand, the overflowing garbage can, a series of burned out light bulbs, and a broken facade or window invite the unwanted user. The maintenance and preservation principles are the most baffling of the four environmental design pillars, connecting with both intended and deviant users on a deeper level. A well-kept structure, plus clean and organized shared areas send a message, we are here, we are responsible, and we are not your next victim.' Acting on the preservation and maintenance plan is the least expensive, an impactful step in creating a safer place.

Additional Considerations

A thorough assessment of risk will ensure the reduction of harm by exposing surprises and previously unknown threats. The formal evaluation is the best teaching and learning opportunity without experiencing a forceful crisis or adverse circumstances. While the topic may be new to most, the components of a formal assessment are too simple to ignore; shedding new light on vulnerabilities and reducing casualties with education.

Awareness of vulnerability offers more than a measure of weakness; recognition of this misunderstood state of mind and environment prevents harm. Most have a bias leaning toward the identification of either vulnerability or strength, and we rarely volunteer to correct the habits in need of repair. We can reach our goal in many ways; those who recognize strengths, weakness, and acknowledge the warnings, are on a safe route. Most important, the path we choose should always include serious contemplation of the Environmental Norm (Dimension One of Predictable Harm). It is from this foundation we see the deviations from the norm; External Clues  (Dimension Two), we sense our Internal Cues (Dimension Three) and notice the Stand-Alone Evidence (Dimension Four); all leading to lifesaving prevention and Rapid Communication (Dimension Five of Predictable Harm).

QuikTip:

"Vulnerability: What does the image project without words?"

As we discussed previously, attitude is the vital ingredient in a harm-free day. Evidence and intuition supported by specific observations keep you on the path. We are usually limited by outside influences, vulnerability hums in the background of every mind, serving as a welcome companion to those who fully understand her purpose. In short, those who follow and act on the vulnerability in their lives WILL side-step risk, a rare blend of courage and fear leading to strength. Those who only 'feel vulnerable' suffer in the zone of higher risk. After assessing the risk, we act without delay. Awareness followed by action is curative; our safety footprint begins with assessment at once followed by new habits.

While seemingly abstract, we have the power to reduce vulnerability if we define it, right-size it, and support the attitude to perfect it. While the mental health community and criminal justice system consider desire in the mind of each offender, we must focus on reducing opportunities for violence, loss, injury, and victimization. The formal risk assessment will clarify the goal, accepting vulnerability as a fact of life and find how to minimize the power it has over our peace of mind and safety.

The components of a formal evaluation may be used as a guide and a teaching template. As mentioned earlier, a simple strategy is a successful strategy, and we plan on keeping this basic. This format is suitable for an assessment of the workplace, church, recreational facility, or even a temporary vacation home. You can choose to increase complexity, add photos or details using this format as the foundation. Our goal at this point is learning a process, which includes an introduction to the basics of a formal risk assessment. It is a method that should be reviewed, customized to specific needs, shared carefully, and applied practically. Most important, the assessment document, once completed, should be kept secure and confidential. A small handful of dangerous people could abuse the information found in the assessment of your selected property.

The Formal Risk Assessment:

This format is currently used by several of my clients, applying the process to private properties, dinner cruises, miscellaneous recreation areas, private airports, construction site safety, educational facilities, offices, and large shopping malls. This risk assessment works as presented or may be improved, creating enhancements and ideas supporting personal and professional safety.

The best rationale for the formal process is education; employees and others involved in a formal risk assessment have a grasp of the principals of exposure and vulnerability. I prefer to hand out up to five clipboards and blank assessment forms during a live evaluation; offering a group learning environment and a team approach. Much like a Chief Financial Officer teaching the basics of accounting to employees and improving fiscal responsibility, those who want a culture of safety may use the formal risk assessment and quickly expand the prevention footprint. I suggest a review of the process and highlights below; consider each category then customize, personalize, and make it work for you. Note: Please use caution when considering the removal of evaluation categories as this physical risk assessment includes the minimal Standard of Care.

Highlights

The Formal Risk Assessment may be used to assess structures, lodging areas, transit collection points, and more. It is a practical approach exposing vulnerabilities and strengths. The final document reduces exposure, and in some cases insurance premiums. Before the assessment, please consider permission or notification of all stakeholders and adjacent property owners. A thorough examination often includes accessing neighboring properties, and they usually appreciate advanced notice. Best practices include a few dry-runs before recording a final report.

The following exercise includes a brief description of each section of the risk assessment. Again, add as needed or include images, but this is the recommended minimum:

A. Critical Concern(s) are those rising to the level of an active threat, a significant natural risk, court-recognized vulnerability or risk factor listed below. If a threat is suspected or has been reported, directly or by a third-party, or if suspicious behavior is suspected. Critical concerns are those which, if not addressed, may place human life or high-value assets in peril. The definition of interests is clarified below. Critical concerns are prominently noted first in the formal assessment so that any person reviewing the document will at once recognize the urgency. In cases of workplace violence reduction, a critical concern triggers specific notifications and possible actions. Example: If an employee reports s/he is the victim of domestic violence or a worker threatened outside the workplace. Both scenarios would trigger a Critical Concern Response and CC Designation (i.e., corporate notification, notify police, EAP, HR, etc.). You will see a similar rating near the end of the formal assessment. Double-handling is intentional.

B. Target name and rating. The target name specific to your property within your scope of influence; a standard designation or normal reference-that is a construction site, post office, home, central office, Park and Ride collection point, recreation center, middle school, delivery truck, and courthouse. The rating (0-100), offers a point of conversation. Rarely below 20 (low-risk), Critical Concerns typically range 80 – 100 (high-risk). A rating of 80 may include a faulty door that cannot be locked. A score of 98 may point to an emergent need, such as a leaking fuel tank.

C. Type of threat or concern in proximity. This evaluation dimension is a sub-set to the last section, a more detailed description of special concerns. A risk may include Domestic Violence Housing, a half-way house for sex offenders, Alzheimer's Care Facility, unusual foot traffic, ammunition storage area, local biohazards, SafePlace Shelter for children, High-Risk Executive Housing, or any other unusual circumstance qualifying as high-risk. Remember, this is a confidential document with limited distribution. Be candid and complete as you list unusual circumstances.

D. Assessor(s) name. For the name and role of the assessor or assessors, for example, Property Manager, Social Services Representative, Insurance Provider, Convention Coordinator, Real Estate Professional, Dorm Captain, Maintenance or Security

Specialist, etc. Again, I recommend a minimum of two people for all assessments.

E. **Category of a possible disturbance.** Why would an offender target you, others, or this location? Or what makes the worksite hazardous? The forecast; reasonable prediction, risk based on many factors, which include the symbolism, inventory, vulnerability, and accessibility of our target or worksite. The risk may include temporary conditions. Recent events, acts of hate, trends or even localized threats may contribute to a reasonably deduced choice. As an example, trends in construction risk include high-value metal or copper theft, remodel work on the home of a high-risk client, and working in an unusually hazardous confined space or soil layered in biohazards. The assessor may highlight one or several items from a customized list based on the trends, and upcoming protests or traffic disturbances. My advice is to select categories that are realistic and possible rather than extreme. To list only extremes could become a barrier. Committees, stakeholders or executives, and the individuals you intend to influence are impressed by a balanced assessment.

F. **Probable motive of disruption.** Another prediction based on information and intelligence known at the time of the assessment. I recently evaluated a conference hall for a religious conference; 2800 attendees planned to occupy a convention center. One-word, hate, describe the probable motive for a disruption. It happened; the haters arrived, and we had a rational response, which the haters hated.

G. **Probable method of disruption.** Again, based on information known at the time of the assessment, to include web-based hacking, traffic interruption, picket or anti-position demonstration, paint-bombs, infrastructure shutdown; water supply, food supply, power or electrical shutdown. In one case, we wondered why the predicted protest never happened. They didn't show up because they trashed the critical infrastructure before the event.

H. **Greatest threat (Internal or External):** This criterion is disturbing but necessary: It asks if we are more at risk due to internal employees, family members or external offenders. Are we more at risk due to employee disputes or because of direct access and unlocked doors? Are we more at risk because of a labor dispute or because of the product we produce, represent, or keep in our storage? Are we at risk due to symbolism, our assets, or a new law or market?

Legal marijuana has changed the lives of many near my home in Washington State. Brilliant entrepreneurs began growing, advertising, and selling some of the best weed in the world (their claim, not mine).; however, they did not prepare for new clientele. The change in clients was and is their greatest threat. They tripled their sale of nachos, self-serve beef jerky, and Hostess brand snack food, and doubled the risk of burglary, theft, loitering and urinating in the parking lot. Many did not forecast for the new threat.

I. High-risk contributing factors. Another forecast: How many could be affected, injured or killed based on the results of the threat and method in the forecast? What property is tempting, will be damaged, and to what extent? How will the event impact other facilities or pedestrian and vehicular traffic flows? I live in a hotbed of specific risks and protests. We know who they are, where they live, and how they think. Threats trending in my area are much different than the forecast near Area 51 in Nevada, threatened fishing vessels off the Oregon Coast, and to the trains delivering waste to the Nuke Dump near Hanford, 300 miles away. One can easily see why all assessments include a customized perspective. Some will be at-risk due to human threats while others are in danger due to weather or landslide.

J. Estimate of immediate economic impact. A monetary estimate of the effects, damage, or casualties because of a disturbance. The amount estimated should be limited to the first impact rather than any cleanup or mitigation. Some of our stakeholders, those who fund our safety, need this number.

K. Closest services: Level 1 trauma center, closest emergency room, decontamination center, and mobile medical, mobile decontamination, Red Cross, language translation services, and the phone number for all the above. Essential items we brainstorm before the crisis; prepare for a minor fire, car accident on your property, and the plane forced to crash in your neighborhood or land on the boss's favorite golf course. Knowing the nearest location of a high-level trauma care center and the best routes, 24-hour emergency room, or emergency care facility is also imperative. I suggest researching what a service can and cannot handle, and if they can respond to your site, and who will coordinate the team on-scene or next to the target.

L. Existing prevention problems: Prevention challenges include any environmental, human, or traffic safety issues elevating risk, calling for added changes to enhance safety, and when the tools, technology, and techniques do not exist. Every risk assessment includes a deficiency, small or large. The big corporation, home, or public organization will have unmet needs due to budget constraints or logistical restrictions. This section may include a shopping list or dream sheet, even if you cannot afford the enhancement to safety. Examples: Traffic barriers, metal detectors, or access control issues such as pedestrian and crowd collection areas or "funnel points" and limited access areas, which may be difficult to access by responders. Nice to have: Updated list of Level 3 Sex Offenders living in your area, portable HazMat decontamination unit, defibrillator unit, list of local work release inmates, and local housing for Mentally Ill Offenders.

M. Expected special equipment requirements, primary and alternate locations for field command and leadership post. Special equipment needs are something we should expect well before the necessity arises. Special equipment needs could include buses, services for children, the disabled and elderly, or facilities for animals. We should also consider special equipment needs for neighboring businesses affected. When considering assembly point issues, keep in mind that primary and secondary site selections are essential. Disaster dynamics may change your formal plan. Water, fuel spills, hazmat issues, and wind direction also have an immediate impact on your assembly points for evacuees. As an important note, don't forget to plan for a primary and secondary command post; the assembly point for those who lead and check-in, which is separate but close to the assembly point for print and broadcast media. Alternative sites are a must have!

N. Primary and alternate access/exit points for emergency medical services (EMS). These entrances and exit points are estimated without knowing facts. History tells us a plan needing changes is better than no plan at all. Again, water, fuel spills, hazmat issues, and wind direction have an impact on the EMS assembly points. Anticipate two or three locations that would be safe and separate from other rally points in your plan.

O. Natural threats. This evaluation dimension includes the reality of the location, history, and forecast. Floods, wildfires, mud or snow slides are considerations we process before others do, even though we cannot accurately forecast the hazard. Example: a business on the shoreline of the Pacific Ocean must plan for a storm surge. Mountain passes must plan for snow slides. 70% of my state must plan for flood or forest fires. We seek a projection based upon structure or assessed area. What is the real threat offered by historical data and current events. Not a pleasant thought but a brilliant, lifesaving prediction.

P. Critical environmental cues: Often similar to Assessment Include the security and safety issue that, if not corrected, could lead to loss of life, serious casualty, or significant property damage or loss. Examples include hazardous chemical storage tanks, direct access to combustibles, access to poisons, security checkpoints rarely staffed, cameras that are inoperable; basically, a large-scale lack of concern when it comes to preparedness.

Q. Crime Prevention through Environmental Design (CPTED) issues, mentioned earlier in this chapter, should be noted in any formal assessment. CPTED issues generally include potential concerns and present threat. Lighting, well-groomed landscaping, signage, and visibility in and out of the location are all examples of a strong CPTED plan. Remember, this is the first line of protection, or hopefully, the opposite of the Criminal Curb Appeal sought by the offender. CPTED makes up the visual profile perceived by the public and potential offenders.

Poor Natural Surveillance (above) The intended user cannot look in and occupants cannot look out. The offender sees this as an opportunity.

R. Property assessment, dangers, and recommendations. This stage of the evaluation includes opinion; 1. Safe, with no recommendations (rare), 2. Safe, with minor recommendations and corrections (most common), and 3. Unsafe, with major proposals and revisions.

S. Other value (financial/political/activism). The value calls for an educated opinion; quantify your observations of the property related to economic impacts or risk, political cost or threat based on the season, and activism impacts based on local community events. A vacation property rental may have no vulnerability; however, occupation or if rented by a controversial leader, the threat may increase. A building or construction site may have negligible risk until activists disagree with the planned occupant. A rural factory is virtually unknown until they discover oil reserves beneath, or Sacred Native History nearby.

One such incident occurred in Thailand after the December 26, 2004 tsunami. With reconstruction efforts underway on the Phuket Peninsula, "Other Value" became clear to those framing replacement businesses and vacation properties. A post-Tsunami effort by activists supporting Sea Turtle nesting areas led to destruction, arson, and human casualties on both sides. After working with representatives, it was obvious no one had predicted a risk, which could have been anticipated through a complete assessment and follow-up.

End of the formal Property Assessment. Congratulations!

You have completed the formal risk assessment related to the property; clear, thorough, comprehensive, and with room to grow and improve. Reminder: The assessment instrument excluded face to face risk. I believe the evaluation should be conducted as soon as possible, and then annually. When a threat changes, reassessment should be done often, and daily in extreme cases. For instance, if the assessment ends with a #2 Rating; Safe, with corrections suggested, it should be done again following the regular schedule. If the evaluation leads to a #3 Rating; Unsafe, corrections needed, it should be assessed immediately after unsafe conditions are corrected.

Refresher: Five Dimensions of Predictable Harm:

1. NORMING: Identification and understanding your stable norm or a safe environment,

2. EXTERNAL CLUES: Useful or unusual evidence of danger; words, equipment, external signals, and potential clues that deviate from all-things-normal,

3. **INTERNAL CUES:** Internal warning signs that depart from your standard feelings of wellness and safety. The gut-check and our natural intuition sensing the not-so-normal,

4. **SOLO OR STAND-ALONE EVIDENCE:** A single warning sign (clue) or internal reaction (cue) making no other evidence necessary. A solo and undeniable threat or conditions, and

5. **SHARED-RISK (rapid communication):** The need for and acting on a rapid communication strategy. Knowing with whom to communicate, when, and why it calls for immediate communication.

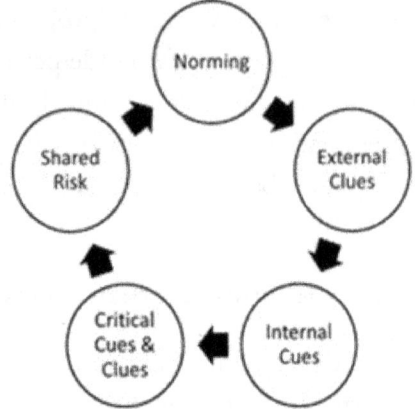

End of Chapter Seven.

CHAPTER EIGHT

Forecasting Face to Face

Chapter eight will address the most difficult challenge thus far; arguably most dangerous, we dedicate the section to predicting and preventing intentional harm, face to face. This may include being trapped or cornered by a miserably agitated and frightening offender. I'll offer ideas, present a solution-based template, and challenge a few assumptions about face-to-face forecasting and rapid intervention. Chapter eight also rolls out de-escalation skills; quiet considerations and the verbal talents needed to calm the agitated and potentially violent.

A Long-List of Alternatives

As I've mentioned previously, this text presents a volume of reliable systems, philosophies, and mental models. The level of ability, awareness, and the choice of tools constitute a decision only you can make. The list of options is too long for wholesale approval. The choices will become your brand over mandatory rules or applications promoted by myself and others. I encourage my students and readers to construct a hybrid. Grasp only those principles fitting the present need, current conditions, and individual taste. I suggest you enact the most impactful lesson first, absorb the meaning in real time, and then come back to the list and select another tool.

Simply told, we often miss the cues and clues of danger that lie ahead. Often oblivious to the risk, we may never realize we have strolled through a hornet's nest without a sting. It might be luck, could be grace, or the statistical norm experienced by many including myself. Skipping through a band of criminals without awareness confirms the most lethal distraction of all; not recognizing danger, rarely knowing what we missed, and how lucky we have been. On a community scale, a pleasant soul has a brush with violence every day with or without notice; the near-miss is part of our daily and nightly routine. I can almost guarantee you've had the undetected brush with calamity, with or without a faint awareness. The exposure is unnecessary when knowledge, talents, and techniques are available and support early warning awareness. I share this only to heighten knowing what we don't know. Feeling safe due to low awareness is not safety at all.

Face to Face: We Start with the End in Mind

Of the many mantras in crisis work, I favor the phrase *start with the end in mind*. The exit strategy should be first on the list in all estimations of risk. Finding an escape route is typically the last thing people consider; however, it is the foundation of most decisions. We always consider the hasty exit before verbal de-escalation begins. Those who engage without an exit strategy often freeze when the stuff hits the fan. Your position in a room, your proximity to the offender, and knowing the exit come first, then verbal mediation. As a career-negotiator, working from a customized van parked hundreds of feet from the threat was the standard. We were armed and hyperalert; however, we still crafted an exit plan and discussed where we would go and what we would do if communication turned violent. Discussing a safe exit was a priority before we knew anything about the offender.

An exit strategy calms the spirit and increases confidence, clearing the way for a clean process. It may sound like paranoia; however, paranoia is an irrational fear. Considering extreme possibilities and a rational response first, is far from irrational. If your role in life includes leadership, protection, and shielding others in a family, you can take pride in your tactical perspective.

Years later, when an argument erupts in public between two or more people, I usually know my exit strategy within seconds. I don't flee, but calmly view the argument and consider my options. The rescue routes of escape might include windows, rear stairs, fire escapes, or the main entry point. Most important, escape options need to be within your limitations and supported by steadfast commitment to act absolutely. Once known, verbal de-escalation is cued up.

Zones of Awareness:

In the case of a human risk assessment, I rely on and teach three zones of enhanced awareness. These territories are natural, social, and distinctly defined, risk interpreted at the most significant distance from a threat and maximized as you close the range with the potential offender.

Zone Three:

Zone three is a managed-risk assessment made with distance up to a short city block or 50 meters away. Once aware of the tools, most students are surprised by the range in which a forecast may begin. I know of cases where the potential victim noticed the offender acting or reacting unusually. They noticed behavior early and it became a life-saving talent. Skills of the potential victim guided the scenario to a successful and safe conclusion.

Example: A prospective offender has crossed the street for no known reason. After noticing he's walking your way, he should be outside or just entering zone three (a significant distance for assessment). You decide to cross the street. Well done! Then the potential offender crosses the road as well. Recognizing a deviation from norm, you shift from casual observations to intentional focus. Those who have supplemental protection (pepper spray or other weapons) should mentally consider its use and where it is located (body, purse, ankle). This will mentally cue-up any related training. If it were me, the weapon would not be displayed, but accessible. We cross the street again, returning to the original walkway. The possible threat is now a considerable concern. Then he crosses the roadway for a second time.

We appropriately suspect something is dreadfully wrong. Once triggered by observation in zone three, the broad perspective provides ample time to collect information and respond strategically. There's no need to wait. The offender has been set-up by your early assessment and movements. The distant snapshot offered in zone three will become a dear friend, allowing a duration of time to make a rational decision. We stop, change directions, flee or otherwise prepare. We'll come back to zone three.

Zone Two:

Zone two observations include a closer look at the potential threat; his clothing, stance, pace, co-conspirators, potential weapons, his focus and view, and why he may be a threat to you and others. Depending on the environment, zone two could be 40 feet away or four car lengths. Once the potential risk enters zone two, observations become detailed, and we have less time to collect information. Our views become stressful and rapid, and our decision to stop, change directions, and flee are urgent. We'll re-visit zone two in a moment.

Zone One:

Stating the obvious, zone one is the highest risk. Our scope narrows and becomes focused, to include consideration of our restrictions and options. We casually scan the subject of our concern, and, in a perfect world, we stop moving toward the threat and keep a minimum distance of 21 feet (6-7 meters). Zone one includes observations of the potential offender's eyes, hands, and feet, as all three could be used as a weapon. Remember, no one has ever been beaten or stabbed from 21 feet. A punch is impossible, a strong-armed robbery improbable, and a purse-snatch, sexual assault or a painful kick to the groin is unheard of from seven yards.

We continue de-escalation techniques in zone one; observations and words become deliberate, precise, and moderated. Our breathing should be regulated to slow and deep respiration, and our posture or physical stance should be sturdy; a non-threatening position is helpful; hands relaxed or folded in front of you and above the beltline. We may hit the Emergency Dial on our mobile phone and ask for help. You already have more than enough information. Call for help! In some cases, we may only have time to push the emergency notification. Pocket the phone at once after dialing.

It's time to breach his cloak of secrecy, call out his behavior, and say *STOP!* Trust the law of averages, he is not expecting any words. Speak loudly, and say it often. *STOP! YES, I'm talking to you. STOP!* Our hands should remain clear of items in close contact, with or without an absolute urgency. We focus on one of three alternatives: A. Flee. Follow the exit strategy you already had in mind. B. Negotiate and de-escalate, as we back out of the situation, or C. If attacked, go on the offensive, get angry, get loud, and use the force necessary to protect yourself and others.

Those with awareness throughout zone two and three, rarely need to rely on physical self-defense. With distance and estimation, we cut risk in half. Potential victims, while rare, may try to walk through the threat. I've interviewed many of the hopeful and confrontational heroes and attended a handful of the related funerals. I advocate self-defense, which includes avoiding the clash when possible. Pondering the life-threatening extremes is unpleasant;

however, those willing to avoid, while able to fight for life as a final consideration, do whatever's needed. But self-protection begins with side-stepping potentially violent scenarios. Fatal encounters from recent history include sad stories of the missed opportunities to avoid violence. I practice and promote avoidance whenever possible; however, encourage self-defense if cornered. If an assault is inevitable or forced, we kick, gouged the eyes, strike the throat, stomped the top of the foot, and detached the testicles if our life depends on justified violence. I suggest you cross the street instead.

Active forecasting never ends, a relaxed engagement in all environments outside of the home. Those who become proficient have conditioned themselves with a natural and predictive algorithm called the five dimensions of harm. Once practiced, the lifesaving template hums in the back of the mind and supports the assessment of both accidental and intentional risks. We continuously refresh our environmental norm until it becomes automatic (dimension #1), followed by our ability to notice the external clues that seem out-of-place (#2). We listen to our gut or the natural internal cues (#3). We calmly watch for solo threats and stand-alone warnings, certain conditions needing immediate action or hasty exit (#4). And we always share our risk, have a rapid communication strategy (#5). We respect the benefits of the unique tools, their message, and advantages offered. At this point in the learning process you may feel like your drenched with data. Don't worry, overwhelm is normal. The process will eventually make sense if you ponder, practice, discuss and apply the new knowledge.

Observed On-Camera:

Before we dive into the details, let's examine how we came up with an extensive list of clues and conclusions. I facilitated a team of like-minded colleagues in compiling the statistical findings and anecdotal leanings of a possible confrontation. In addition to reports, the FBI National Academy Library and staff, and interviews

No Further Harm: A Purely Predictable Path

previously listed, we viewed and interpreted recorded work-product linked to well-placed Closed-Circuit-Television (CCTV) Cameras. These non-threatening public devices caught serious threats while posted throughout the inner city, rural communities, and transit stations serving subways, buses, and surface trains. The best, most active and balanced-activity cameras were selected and suggested by transit authorities and active peace officers. Once sites were selected, we dedicated time to the review of over 1200 hours of CCTV data, which captured moderate risk environments.

Note: While the locations are not confidential, it would be counterproductive to share precise points on the map. I have agreed to avoid creating a geographical record or the interesting list; precise locations have been omitted, potentially frustrating those prone to extreme travel locations. Recordings, resources, and live CCTV contributors include the USA, Scotland, Ireland, England, Australia, Germany, South America, and a few locations in South Africa. To respect the law of averages, we purposely avoided cameras in historically high-crime areas.

The activity met the primary goal of the CCTV-based research, plus some. We have a better understanding of those recognizing or missing the clues of predictable harm, and successful de-escalation during face to face interactions. The cultural, racial, financial and gender-based identifiers have been removed, creating a data stream of purely human-based behavior. Conclusions and shared signs of danger included actual crimes observed, verbal disputes, and property damaged during fits of rage. We recorded those mesmerized by hand-held devices, walking directly into people and over others. We reviewed car bumpers dented and saw a few fists broken during traffic disputes. Research revealed encounters between strangers, drivers, and employees rather than domestic violence or alcohol-fueled fights in taverns, bars, and public areas known for raw drunkenness and brawling.

We excluded domestic situations. While extremely important, domestic violence situations deserve independent study and probably a dedicated text. Excluding self-defense, all acts of violence are wrong, and domestic violence within the home is horrible; however, the complexities of love, hate, and battles within the castle are inappropriate for this book.

Alcohol-related disputes and drunken riots in or near a sports arena also deserve our attention; however, the violence doesn't meet the threshold for this text. The physical and emotionally-charged arena-activity include an assumption of risk; those confined within a fence, consuming alcohol, and saturated in a contagion of athletics often equal a condensed rivalry. Sporting events throw off the average and offer little value in predictable harm. Violence within the crowd-culture is common; conditions of event-contagion deserve a different study, book, and audience. Scanning the fans during a Monster Truck Rally or Cage Fighting may produce results, however, I find it exhausting and irrelevant in predicting day-to-day hazards. Finally, and without condemnation, the combination of five or more humans, ego, competition, adrenaline, planned rivalry, and inhibitions lowered by alcohol or design, point to elevated risk which is not a forecast, but often an expectation.

With the completion of the CCTV study, this chapter on face-to-face interaction and related cues and clues of violence was nearly complete. CCTV data added to existing police experience and reports, plus helpful information from court records, inmate interviews, and victim advocates. We relied on a fat file of crisis negotiation notes, workplace violence prevention stories, and evidence provided by survivors. With the help of a relatively diverse group of safety practitioners, we compiled enough data to round out the details needed to predict and prevent harm. Also added to the list, successful de-escalation techniques, and body language via camera, added a surprising bonus. While I avoid the publication of negative habits, we also observed dismal de-escalation failures by women and men on and off the professional clock. To the positive, we found thousands of people interacting with ease, caution, and courtesy.

Often painfully dull, the CCTV study would complete the puzzle; hours of nothingness, productive and predictable patterns of those intending to harm an innocent victim, and those potential offenders who halted their behavior and aborted their criminal scheme. Stated differently, I was blessed to capture incomplete street crimes as they evolved, spontaneous violence that was entirely avoidable, and examine why a criminal offense may have been nullified moments before harm or attack. I've done my best to discard questionable conclusions and capture only the most obvious examples.

You're about to discover why the bad guy often stops before his attack and why potential victims, equipped with the skills to forecast harm, often remain unscathed. I found predictable behavior, clues, and the use of tactical communication; specific words, and other habits and verbiage during de-escalation.

Prediction & Prevention Up Close:

I continue to emphasize the deviant formula for violence is predictable and can be interrupted. Prevention needs early detection and a little guesswork; we avoid harm with our best prediction, and the forecast includes imperfect human interpretation. Innocent mistakes are part of complicated situations, unpackaged with clear observations, quick decisions, and prompt communication. Our estimates of danger will include incorrect details, the flawed forecast is enough when compared to the average state of bliss others enjoy. If your evaluation of risk frustrates others, I suggest you apologize for any ill-will and continue to predict. Being wrong is part of learning how to do it right.

The world is complete with people who prefer ignorance rather than taking a risk by judging the danger posed by others. Those who reject the skills of judgment rarely buy a book promoting the avoidance of predictable and preventable harm. While I choose a different approach, I respect the choice. Forecasting harm is a life-saving effort, not a perfect science. Prevention always includes two risks; the risk of harm, and the risk in making an educated assessment.

Recognition & Avoidance

Human observations and the study of those around you will lead to a change in behavior, movements, and habits. Acting in good faith, you may decide to stop walking, move, run, say something assertive, cross the street unexpectedly, or choose to exit or skip the elevator. If this offends someone, you have offended for all the right reasons. History includes those injured after omitting an assertive boundary or skipping the decision to alter the original plan or route.

When we understand the components of harm, we are equipped to define, defend, or discuss our actions and reactions. At best, we can describe exactly why we responded as we did, and, at a minimum, we qualify our trusted intuition as the driving force. I have never met a client or past student that had to apologize for seeking a safe space. Most important, we begin with a peaceful mindset. We are seeking safety, low drama, and less stress. We forecast risk for all the right reasons.

Establishing awareness of your environmental norm is personal. Recognition and awareness of tone, cleanliness, and hazards will vary by region, climate, and individual vulnerability. My current norm includes parking in downtown Seattle, walking four blocks, and waiting on a public sidewalk until I gain access to my current client. The norm includes traffic, business activity, and specific panhandlers I know by name. A drug dealer works the alley off 1st Avenue, interesting coffee conversations take place at Westlake Center, and the sidewalk near the Union Gospel Mission is packed with people. If cycling, the norms on the route include wet cobblestone near Alaskan Way, brutal railroad tracks on Elliot Avenue, and a flurry of supply trucks reversing into loading ramps and waterfront restaurants. I know the risk, the norm, and I recognize changes. I've absorbed the sounds, smells, peak usage periods, and the progress of each construction project. The observations do not enhance my fear, quite the opposite. My blood pressure drops while norming. My norms and routines are much different than employees at SeaTac International Airport. The norm is different for those painting the Golden Gate Bridge, manufacturing homes, and for employees at Mayo Clinic.

The world gets more interesting after norming the environment. A flood of observations may be enjoyable or a tad much. Some deviations from the norm will become obvious. The mismatch of clothing and temperature, gestures, body mechanics, pace and volume often jump off the page of life. That awkward rage from an unknown person, unconscious habits, and you may notice the sickening sweet tone of a stranger about to take advantage of you or a colleague. Risk reveals itself in subconscious evidence, followed by expressions and unusual words that deviate from the norm ever so slightly. While many assessments examine facial proof, you are becoming a professional, scanning and soaking in much more. Body clues advance the message of intentional acts; warning that a person or group are about to do something they are naturally hesitant to do. Even the worst of society have a conscience or hope to avoid detection of immoral or unhealthy behavior, and the evidence shows up before the act.

QuikTip:

"When in doubt, promptly point it out. Be wrong for all the right reasons."

Body-clues; expression, eyes, hands, and even the feet provide a window into the person's mind, telling us a short-story about their current emotional state. Body language is an early-warning device built into every human being. In short, the way a person carries themselves gives us valuable insight as to whether they stand for a threat or not. It's time to add a few assets and tips to your mental toolbox:

Humans Assessing Humans:

A. The Human Face (Zone 1 & 2 Assessment)

The face is the most reliable, expressive, rapid, and interactive glimpse; a living image presented close-up and difficult to alter, hide, or misuse. The face is a human radiator, an interactive display, and a visible mosaic of uncharted clues waiting to be read. The face can be manipulated, however doing so without detection is a tough task. Those feigning a facial gesture are obvious, embarrassing in some cases. Some experts can control facial expressions. I've managed undercover narcotics officers who do it and met some FBI operatives and CIA agents who must, or risk losing their lives. Sales professionals, trial attorneys, and many politicians have majored in minor facial manipulation and do it well. My ex-mortgage banker seemed to go face-neutral with ease while tacking on unnecessary fees. But when I challenge myself to look beyond the conventional, even the most conditioned and stoic face will supply new evidence.

In some cases, they lose all color, filling in with a rosy-red glow in others, and occasionally twitching mildly when tested. We recognize the change, pause, respond differently with facts beyond the words. While entertaining, non-violent Broadway actors, sales experts, and the candidate for mayor are not our concern or focus. Reading the face of a potential offender is the goal in this short section. The expression and evidence found above the neck, while only one part of the full forecast, offers a crucial estimation we cannot afford to miss. Often fun, and occasionally hilarious, our goal is serious; lower injury and save lives.

The facial appearance of those who intend to harm is telling; the

No Further Harm: A Purely Predictable Path

lower body-language rarely matches their face. Consider the head fake of a professional basketball player; looking to the left and passing the ball to a player on the right. The extreme example of the mismatch between body and facial behavior, one that still surprises the viewers, holds limited success with other NBA players. Those who entertain the possibility of a head fake as they run the hardwood, usually receive the throw with ease and master the play. Those who discount or dismiss the surprise, typically miss the pass or get slammed by an embarrassing, painful, and humiliating ball to the side of the head. The difference between success and painful loss is an awareness of the probabilities. Within the context of predictable harm facial interpretation has lifesaving benefits, a rare skill accessible to those who are still open to the possibilities.

Remember, aggression equals increased blood pressure, obvious respirations, and an elevated pulse, which may be visible in the neck, on the forehead, or near the temples. The offender may try to control his reactions but rarely succeeds in curtailing spontaneous perspiration, flaring nostrils, rapid blinking or a fixed stare. His dry mouth also signals distress as his tongue sticks and words become difficult. He can't get enough oxygen and begins taking in large breaths of air or quickly breathing through both his nose and mouth. Trust the facial read and your gut. While your reactions may be intrusive, assume you are correct and remain focused on his features or your swift retreat.

Most balanced adults smile when necessary, stare or look away as needed, but the whole body doesn't cooperate when a person holds a devious or secretive plan to harm, steal and lie. The mismatch, a deviation from the norm, suggests an internal conflict. The new and nervous sniffle, clearing the throat, nose-pulling (light pinching of the tip of the nose with the thumb and index finger), earlobe tugging or pinching offer clues. A sudden need to rub the eyes, self- grooming any facial or head hair, plus throat and chin rubbing expose the internal menace. My advice is to stay calm and study the face, while peacefully scanning the whole-body posture. When, why, and how often these habits start and end often suggest a problem. We must consider recent history, as in a few seconds or minutes from the past. We compare the changes, the timeline, and the context of the expression.

A Micro-Flash of The Eyes

Specific to the facial read and worthy of the lifesaving honor roll, Target Glance has saved my bacon. I also believe I missed the target glance offered by James before the vehicular assault described earlier. Target Glance includes two parts:

1. Telegraph the intention of the offender, and

2. As a deviation from the norm; the eyes or glance do not fit the behavior of the hands, feet, and other body mechanics.

The unconscious shift of the eyes is often a mismatch to the point of interest. In these cases, our intuition usually kicks in first, creating angst and confusion; and we rarely trust this wise internal advice. Trust me; internal advice is unusual and astute advice, the gut level advisor (dimension three) of predictable harm. These feelings are often counter-culture, needing judgment, freezing the moment, and muting physical reaction or verbal expression. My advice includes accepting rather than rejecting the automatic flash.

Target Glance - Telegraphing:

The first of these twin-assets, telegraphing, is a frequent flyer. Consider a factual incident starting with an awkward and escalating scenario in a favorite family restaurant. In this excerpt from a real-life drama on CCTV, emotion and distress were on the rise over the price and quality of a meal. The manager became the default target of frustration. Civility left the conversation, and while the offender had been staring into the manager's eyes during his extreme disgust, and even on a grainy recording, we saw the strange glance.

The first flash caught our attention but meant nothing. The second shift of his eyes seemed unusual, and the third was enough, creating a natural rush to fight, flee, or remain frozen. The manager froze while experiencing the subconscious impact of Target Glance. The fourth flash of the customer's angry eyes confirmed a rapid glance toward a steak knife on an unoccupied table in the restaurant. Considering the entire interaction, which lasted less than 90 seconds, it was fair to assume the knife was in the offender's plan. It was a correct assumption, the victim missed or rejected the target glance, and the blade speared into the victim. He survived the attack, and the offender was arrested. The manager missed the clue or didn't have the training and knowledge needed to give it meaning.

Telegraphing intentions via the unconscious use of Target Glance should alter your fight to be right; you respond by creating distance, time, and you fire up your best brand of de-escalation. Based on your observations, a mental and a physical shift to safety, and the deliberate use of de-escalation technique will save at least one life, and possibly more. Good news! A reliable prediction is available, and the proper response is distance, based on the forecast of potential violence via the telegraph of Target Glance.

Target Glance and Context:

While working in uniform, I've had offenders' glance at my holstered handgun two or three times in rapid succession. Glancing at a Peace Officer's holstered gun is not necessarily a terrible thing. The flash of eye movement is crucial when it starts immediately after the offender learns of a warrant for his arrest. The context blended with the micro-shift of an offender's eyes is no longer a matter of mutual interest in firearms. The meaning changed because the context changed, which at once changes the urgency related to his glance toward the holstered gun. One recent case seen on CCTV unfolded in precisely this fashion. The offender learned of the threat to his freedom and revealed his potential intention in at least four micro-flashes of Target Glance. He lunged toward the officer's gun, and, thank God for an internal predictive algorithm; the officer was one step ahead. The offender failed.

In other cases, the offender looked at a window, paused, and dove through it. A bad guy made several micro-glances at a vehicle, then carjacked an innocent victim, and used the car to flee an assault. In a busy shopping area, the offender shifted his glance toward a purse placed inches from a victim who was writing a check. The targeted victim noticed the glance and a slow step by the suspect. He received a nasty stab wound to the back of his hand, and a permanent spot-tattoo in his flesh; Bic Brand, broad-tipped medium-blue ink.

In a more frightening case, the offender continuously glanced a child standing in the lobby of a theater. The child walked into the theater bathroom without a guardian, and the offender followed. Offenders have glanced at vases, ceramic ashtrays, large rocks, golf clubs, baseball bats, goldfish bowls, and frozen meat before using the item as a weapon. Yes, a frozen chicken used as a weapon and a very destructive tool, which knocked the victim into a state of temporary confusion.

A personal favorite, which includes a lovely conclusion, highlights the power of the eyes as a clue in preventing harm and a serious offense. In this case, the offender micro-flashed a few glances toward the parking lot while standing at the counter of a small convenience store. Mr. K, a well-respected shop owner, trained in forecasting harm, caught the flash of target glance. The offender had approached the counter requesting smaller bills for a 100-dollar note. He fumbled through his wallet and pockets, apparently struggling to find the high-value cash note without success. The offender's glance toward the main doors and parking area started as he searched for the 100-dollar bill he didn't have. It appeared to be a ruse or a delay, and Mr. K was not going to wait for a conclusion. He responded once he had enough information rather than ALL the information. The target glance added to the unusual request, was a substantial deviation from the typical environment. With the push of a button, Mr. K auto-locked all access points; back door, side door, and the main front doors locked with the sound of a low buzz and a snap.

Mr. K left the confused "customer," walked to the backroom and storage area, and asked his spouse to join him "for a break." Taking a break was code for "we have a problem." Both entered a safe-room, locked the door, and called 9-1-1. While one offender fled, the primary bad-guy was still trying to break out of the store when police officers arrived and made the arrest. The scenario did not go as planned; the offender's frustration peaked when the co-defendant and the gun needed for the robbery were too slow to enter the convenience store. The armed part of an armed robbery had been locked out of a crime needing a gun. Thanks to an astute and brave Mr. K, who noticed a deviation from the norm, he had peacefully interrupted a severe crime, thanks to context and the glance.

Target Glance - Telegraphing offers a glimpse into the future as offenders flash a glance toward the other offender you may be unaware of, a glance toward the path they intend to use when they flee, and the high-value mobile device momentarily unattended. They may glance at security cameras with their head lowered, and they flash a glance repeatedly at a single victim they have selected for assault. Those who catch the clue, avoid the harm.

Target Glance – Relevance:

In the second part of the meaning, we consider the significance of shifting eyes away from the principle point of interest. The clue is difficult to detect as the offender takes his eyes off the natural point of interest or where he should be focused. All body mechanics suggest he's reading a magazine or examining his smartphone; that is, everything but the eyes. Hollywood intentionally relies on irrelevant eye direction to increase either suspense or mystery of a subject acting the mini-drama. Dramatic and award-winning entertainment often rely on the use of a man seated on a park bench reading a newspaper. The camera pans in for a close-up, and the audience discovers a suspicious man, who is not reading but looking beyond the paper. The paper is a cover for the actor as he spies or otherwise surveys covertly from the park bench. The professional Hollywood set-up hits the mark and heightens the internal cue of suspicion in thousands of viewers.

Target Glance - Relevance also applies in shoplifting cases. The offender holds a product as if he's reading the label. Everything appears normal; responsibly holding an expensive item in his hand, he only seems to peruse the description or the contents. The tell includes target glance; he's not reading the label. Everything lines up except for the eyes, which glance at potential barriers to his crime, witnesses, and everywhere but the label or item poised inches from his nose. Most adults miss the strange habit, looking at the item of interest rather than the eyes. Those trained in forecasting harm bypass the item and stick with the facial read.

Important in understanding the significance of a micro-flash, Target Glance earned respect while my team was tracking Sexually Violent Predators in the mid-1990s. The mall was an exciting and surprising laboratory as we monitored and observed Level 3 Predators who had slithered their way out of jail legally but prematurely. The mall had always been a healthy place to test the assessment skills of new officers; however, I was surprised to find sexual predators testing their urges post-release. While a new and creepy revelation, the pedophile offered live-lab examples of Target Glance as he walked the mall for hours at a time. His glance included a bias toward children; nine out of ten, to be exact. Despite the mass of beautiful adults, food courts, and exciting items in the mid-mall kiosk, the predator-pedophile target-glanced children fitting his preference 90% of the time. Hardly scientific proof, but highly persuasive evidence in the reliability of Target Glance. The facial feature aligned with the offender's record of assaulting children.

No Further Harm: A Purely Predictable Path

Forecasting harm does not require knowing the intricate details of the offenders' intentions. We only seek the cues and clues leaning toward a deviation from the norm. Something doesn't fit, and we respond with care, protection, and further observation. Target Glance has saved my life and the life of other safety-minded friends. In many cases, we didn't know what was wrong. We recognized something didn't fit; the early warning created a life-saving, injury-reducing pause; a hazard light calling for more preventative action and information.

For the proper assessment of risk, we must ask ourselves, do the facial mechanics fit the current environment? When did the expression change, why did the quirks (deviations from the norm) start, why did the stare replace a comfortable and diffused eye contact, and what other evidence suggests a warning? In most cases, excluding the rare exposure to a clinical psychopath, the human fight, flight or freeze-response cannot be managed, regulated or hidden. While an aggressor can remind himself to remain calm, expressions and body mechanics rarely cooperate.

Read Clues, Sense Cues

Remember, forecasting should be a guilt-free application of natural skill. The bad guy has a problem, not you, a potential victim. Holding a deviant thought of illicit intention leaks out, and you can catch it and use it to your safe advantage. In the world of No Further Harm, power shifts to the potential victim. The only possible exception to a reliable forecast is the psychopath. This is a rare encounter, and according to my mentors, they represent 2% of the population, and those are often non-violent psychopaths. Only 2% can hide behind a mask of sanity or the poker face when planning a deviant scheme or when challenged with the truth. After thousands of encounters, I can confidently say I have met only one psychopath capable of maintaining quiet body language and neutral facial gestures in opposition to those expected. Wesley Allen Dodd, a serial killer I interviewed for many hours before the execution, could control his nonverbal gestures. But even Mr. Dodd, while successfully suppressing gestures, could not hide a bright red rash on his neck and inner-forearms as he pondered violent thoughts.

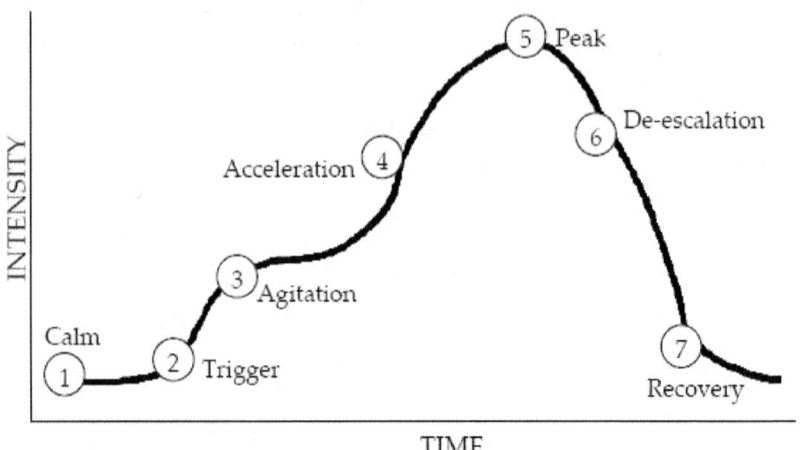

When the motive is flawed the body talks, the face cracks, and the clues are generally available to those aware of the evidence found in predictable harm. The main point and a challenging shift include a necessary change in our attitude and how we respond to first observations. Most will rationalize a good reason for the facial behavior and other clues of a potential offender. Our safety calls for the opposite approach in our evaluation. If you know the person, you may feel safe enough to verbalize the observations, openly asking about visible reactions. If the threat is unknown, and he often is, we respond by creating immediate distance. We move on, away, or make an excuse to create distance, time, and a safe space.

At the beginning of my career, I would search my heart to rationalize the best possible justification for a deviant facial read; a menu of empathic denials and compassionate possibilities rolled through my head. Compassion is the typical response for the new student, an acceptable and healthy acknowledgment in any wholesome and fair environment. We're not preparing for a fair exchange or encounter. This text does not promote forecasting techniques in church or during a relaxing family meal at home. If forecasting in either location, reconsider your living conditions and where you worship.

In the great unknown or as environmental clues elevate risk, we should ask ourselves immediate and silent questions: What are my hazards, should I avoid this person, what is my best avenue of escape, and what is the best response? If the person is unknown to you or the facial read is radical or dramatic in comparison to the norm, creating distance will ensure your safety, and override any need to remain and de-escalate. If he follows you, closes space or becomes more aggressive, make noise, scream and attract others to your concerns. You will often get immediate help from local heroes. If incorrect, you were wrong for all the right reasons.

As the offender considers his destructive plan, he knows his thoughts create a threat for you; however, he thinks most about the threat to his freedom. His internal menace raises his heart rate and dilates his pupils, limiting his peripheral vision. His thoughts and physical reactions often create an opportunity to escape. If you decide to flee, consider the position of the offender, a temporary distraction, then escape at a helpful angle; leaving the risk at a hard 90-degree angle from his left or right shoulder, taking advantage of his flawed peripheral vision.

Unlike Hollywood may typify, he is not likely to follow a resistant, screaming threat to his freedom. He usually moves on to a more vulnerable, passive and untrained victim. These are the trivial things offering a lifesaving difference between those who survive and those who stay frozen in fear. Potential victim no more! You are becoming empowered and empowered equals an unattractive victim

B. Below the Head, Face, and Neck (Zone 2 and 3 Assessment):

In low conflict environments, the shoulders are naturally in a comfortable pose as it is too demanding and unnatural to do otherwise. As risk rises, so do the shoulders of some offenders. Uptight thoughts create inflated pressure, shoulder height, and reduced flexibility. Watch for tension, and you may notice unusual body mechanics as the offender turns his whole torso to see rather than just the head and neck. Also, those becoming agitated will often start a subconscious ritual in stretching the neck, shoulders or back. The shoulders offer another opportunity to recognize increased respiration and or the preview of a future strike by hand or fist.

While keeping your hands above the beltline projects readiness, the offender's hands floating around his waistband represent a threat. It's important to watch the hands closely, remembering clinched fists are a deviation from the norm and a sign of aggression. Stretching, popping knuckles during a conversation, or tightly folding his arms are not the habits of a passive person. Hands in the pockets may not be a problem; however, what they have in their hand as it exits the pocket may create a serious dilemma.

I've found that a single hand in pocket, versus two-hands-two-pockets, presents a threat as this is abnormal; humans favor both pockets when trying to remain warm or habitually using their pockets for any reason. In the escalating environment, a single hand in a pocket as the other hand is still animated, often stands for a weapon or contraband. If talking and using hands to aid in his communication, it is highly unusual for the offender to place a single hand into a single pocket unless he has a less than honorable plan.

Below the Waist and Beyond (Zone 2 and 3 Assessment):

The observation of legs and feet offer helpful information in the assessment of predictable human behavior and harm. Trade secret: Observations should begin before its obvious to the offender. We should make our evaluation at a distance qualifying as Zone 2 or 3, described above. Remember, distance equals time, and time equals safe and prompt decisions. While most students find the new material awkward, I've included the offender methodologies of stalking, moving, and trying to follow others. Hopefully, it will support the message of predictable harm. Some of these observations will manifest in the danger zone, Zone 1. As you practice in the lab-of-life, you should begin noticing the clues at a greater distance. Unconventional indicators include the position of the offender's legs and feet while stable, and how they use those feet and legs in following a victim; the mocking pace, deviant pace, and the stalking pace.

Legs, Feet, Pace (Zone 1, 2, and 3 Assessment):

Mocking Pace

This is the most popular follow by our street-level offender. The mocking pace is just what the tag implies, mirroring that of the victim. His pace accelerates, slows, or stops as needed. The offender may look around for no discernible reason, but he is usually tracking or trolling for potential victims. One casual glance cannot detect the mocker. Watch him for thirty seconds, and you will recognize him as a deviation from the norm. Regardless of the offender's skill-set, he's a risk and worthy of avoidance. A simple question or accusation will threaten his cloak of secrecy. Those relying on a mocking pace avoid confrontation.

Deviant Pace

The deviant pace is most erratic, including drafting, walking or running with the sole purpose of, well, we don't always know. He may be tracking a specific victim, real or imagined. Those in the deviant pace usually keep a safe distance to avoid detection. Any observer will reveal his foolishness as a deviation from the norm. Rarely a direct threat, he's obvious to third-parties and an embarrassment to seasoned street crooks. Unlike the stalker or the mocker, internal demons may fuel the deviant pace. He may have started his day with a sinister plan, but he's not particularly good at anything. Covert surveillance is not his specialty. That said, he is often suffering with mental illness, which elevates risk of the unconventional flavor. Don't antagonize those in a deviant pace as they are unpredictable in a confrontation.

The Stalking Pace

The stalking pace includes following, tracking, and forced teaming (core concept #4), most dangerous of the three. The stalking pace includes walking and stopping abruptly. He may slow to a stroll, look around, and take a few casual steps in the opposite direction. His occasional 180 degree turn acts as a detection system; his behavior often unmasks anyone trying to follow him. Any offender using countersurveillance is dangerous.

The stalker plans on surprise encounters or the "accidental meeting." His chance-meetings are often found to be intentional. The stalking pace includes malice and boldness. While deviant follows and mockers prefer secrecy, those engaged in the stalking style are prepared with a preconstructed lie. They will act surprised to see you, rationalize their location before being asked, and some will go on the offense. Some stalkers have asked why you, the victim, is following him, the offender. With an excuse loaded and ready to fire, the offender may be reckless, blatant, and even cocky. These toxic offenders often wear a mask of sanity with pride. Those who stalk are usually confrontational if challenged.

Verbal De-escalation

We conclude the human assessment with de-escalation techniques, miscellaneous tips, information, and warnings. As I mentioned earlier in the text, consider customizing a program most beneficial for you and your closest peers, co-workers and loved ones. Highlight the most proper actions, tips, words, behaviors, and comfortable tells. Select items and evidence based on need rather than entertainment; tools, tactics, and de-escalation techniques that stretch your ability and fill in your gaps or needs.

The eight stages below work best for me and others in crisis work. The stages are based on principles with a broad allowance for individual style. Pay close attention to the strategic use of questions, time, and silence. Remember, start with the end in mind. Know your exit strategy before fully engaging the offender.

Stage 1: Rage and Recognition: The starting point, often characterized by increased conflict, volume, profanity, interruptions. We define our role in the conversation. An introduction and stated purpose, "I'm here to help as a mediator, negotiator, problem-solver, or to restore the peace."

Stage 2: Relief: This phase of diffusing intends to remove urgency from the conversation. We let the offender know we can talk all day or all night, and our intentions are positive. We begin asking questions, avoiding statements and accusations. We start effective use of the pause, allowing a natural gap to develop between comments by the offender and our questions. We let him fill in the blanks. Tactical communication allows the offender to burn-off extra fuel in the form of physical, emotional and mental energy.

Stage 3: Rename: This is often the most dangerous portion of face to face de-escalation. The offender will experience elevated fear grasping the honeymoon may be over. We attempt to create a calm reality, sticking with questions, not statements, and allowing him time to respond.

QuikTip:

"Resolving a hot conflict takes time. Avoid the premature ultimatum."

Stage 4: Amending: Addressing the offender's perceived isolation. We continue to insert progressively more positive resolutions. We prop up the offender and recognize his ability to contribute to a peaceful conclusion. Affirming their value, edging out their fatalistic thinking, we begin painting a compelling image of the future, which includes the offender.

Stage 5 Reframing: involves minimizing drama and shifting to a probable solution. In a perfect world, this is the stage where we refuse to return to the original problem — all resolutions.

Stage 6: Teaming: We try to reduce any lingering space between the communicator and the offender. We try to leverage relationship capital if appropriate, and when possible.

Stage 7: Exit: This is also a risky step if the other stages were not entirely effective. The exit stage suggests the scenario has an end. Stage seven allows essential timelines, the uptick of urgency toward a healthy conclusion, and may normalize natural closure. I suggest phases such as "We need to wrap this up peacefully," or "Let's call it good." "We've had a good conversation. I'm tired and need to take a break." We begin suggest discomfort in continuing, signifying the offender will benefit by. consideration. The exit strategy may include time limits or facts to encourage a prompt resolution.

Stage 8: Reconnection and Closure: (optional) The unique nature of this stage, while optional, is a personal favorite. I used this little trick over the years to lower re-offense and my own anxiety. Crisis negotiations and tough interactions can stack up, the accumulation of offenders was daunting at times. I countered the distress with reconnection and closure. We reconnect with the offender 48 hours after the incident and before 72 hours have passed. We normalize the relationship by checking in. Naturally, we only do this in the correct environment, with support, and if the offender agrees. In most cases, this strategy lowers angst and elevates confidence. It often ends with a handshake.

Miscellaneous Tips & Advantageous Clues

No Further Harm: A Purely Predictable Path

Tips:

a. Communication can lead to violence or prevent harm; we start and end wars with dialogue, which is a moment by moment decision in how you will use your words and silence.

b. Respect is disarming at every stage of a conflict.

c. One may be assertive and respectful simultaneously.

d. Avoid statements during de-escalation and rely on questions.

e. Your political, religious, and assorted pet peeves should be put on hold, maximizing a clean assessment and response.

f. When the offender introduces a weapon, he rarely believes he may lose the gun to a smart tactician posing as a victim.

g. If taken hostage, comply as needed but never enter the victim-mindset; submission is a reasonable, temporary delay and a tactic that buys time and safety.

h. Never escalate: Assert, read, forecast, predict and de-escalate.

Additional Clues & Tells:

As situations may and often do, words reach the threshold of violent thoughts (Remember, Energy Follows Thought); we mentally process all clues and indicators. There are often discrete signs or tells you can rely on; a clue may instruct you to act as you continue to de-escalate.

Fulltime Awareness Advice:

1. Proximity: The distance of at least two arms lengths is the bare minimum to support a level of safety.

2. Posture: How you stand when person-to-person; conferring respect while staying safe and appearing sturdy.

3. Voice and Vocabulary: The tone of a voice has a norm, and therefore deviations from the pattern can be recognized. Volume is the most popular change; however, vocabulary and word structure also change in the eroding conversation. Short words, incomplete sentences, use of profanity relate to a level of perceived threat or defeat. Redundant words and volume say the person is getting angry and believes he's not heard. We keep our distance or step back.

4. Cadence or Pace: The rate of an approach and the pace of our utterances can be telling; urgency, rapid words, and the speed of the walk toward you estimate the intensity of the person. A slow and continuous step, quiet or moderated words are rarely the habits of a dangerous soul.

Possible Clues of Escalation:

1. Ultimatums are aggressive (do this, or else).
2. Popping knuckles, flexing/stretching is often a sign of distress.
3. A fist pronounces tension.
4. Lips moving (without words) is a clue of elevated risk.
5. Walking away, and an immediate return is often aggressive.
6. Hands on hips is a forerunner to full disagreement.
7. Rolling up shirt sleeves during discussion says angst.
8. Overuse of paraphrasing may be aggressive, considered mockery.
9. A lowered chin often precedes an attack.
10. Rubbing, stroking hands are indicators of risk.
11. Relaxed eye contact shifting to a fixed-stare is a hazard.
12. When the face goes red and eyebrows rise, risk elevates.
13. Stretching, popping knuckles or neck is not passive.
14. Threat increases as the space between the feet expand.
15. Raising the chin is often a power-play.
16. An increase of toe or heel tapping is often escalation or angst.
17. Offenders rarely light a cigarette before an attack.
18. Flicking an unfinished cigarette is a pre-attack indicator.
19. Looking away from a victim may be a ruse. Carefully consider the

proximity of the offender before looking toward his interests.

De-escalation includes the creation of a delay. Any delay in harm is considered de-escalation. De-escalation does not always prevent violence; however, it affords the tactical (deliberate) decision-making and mental processing time for both the negotiator and the offender.

De-escalation also allows a quick evacuation of the uninvolved victims and employees. I've been amazed by the high number of innocent victims who made it to safety during a one or two-minute pause in the violence. Delay, not surrender, becomes the most reliable indicator of successful de-escalation. If you have engaged the offender, and he hits the pause button or does not injure others, strong de-escalation is underway and attributed to you. It can be both terrifying and gratifying as the offender slows or stops his path of destruction based on your skills.

In formal hostage negotiations, we often insert a "Surrender Ritual." Unpacking a messy situation and helping our offender resign from his scenario with no further harm is stressful and technical. What the Hollywood depiction does not mention are the various delay tactics used in cooling the environment; we have usually inserted hours of de-escalation via delay before we begin educating the offender in the more exceptional skills of surrender. You are successful when time, even a short duration, passes without violence.

The tipping point leading to de-escalation, the redline or threshold calling for tactical (deliberate) communication, presents itself in many ways. There is, however, seven frequent flyers; indicators begging for outside help before the explosion of emotion and violence, including:

1. Unassigned Rage: He cannot or will not name a source of anger.

2. Wholesale Rejection: A shift to silence, full-time rudeness, or

anti-everything.

3. Odd References to Time: "Do it while you can, everyone will know soon, it won't matter next week, and my point is about to be made."

4. New Pronouns: We to me, they to you, and unusual extremes (everybody is against me, nobody listens, a school full of idiots, the world sucks).

5. Gallows Grandiosity: Small irritations become disdain for the universe.

6. Third-Party Reporting: Urgent concerns reported by clients/customers/family.

7. Pace: An increase in bold words, exaggerated movement, or increased references to violence.

It is important to remember we are conditioned, once under the weight of critical stress levels, to flee, fight, or freeze. In a perfect world, we train and watch for the environment calling for immediate flight, the conditions forcing a fight, and by training, we avoid the ever-popular reaction of freezing.

The art and science of de-escalation include many variables; the advice in this section reflects only the basics. It will be up to the individual to research, practice, and craft the best model of de-escalation; style blended with courage, skills of mediation and diffusing are the profoundly personal skills developed over time.

Situational Questions:

What should we do when faced with a situation calling for verbal intervention?

What should we watch for and what sequence do we follow?

How would we quickly retreat from the situation and where is the closest or quickest way out?

Who will be talking first? I've witnessed several live scenarios with four or five individuals screaming simultaneously at one offender. It would be humorous if it hadn't ended tragically; a price we pay when we forget to train for the single voice and name a primary communicator. Two or more communicating at once equals confrontation rather than de-escalation.

Finally, have law enforcement officers been notified? A call should be made in the preliminary stages of intervention whether the police are needed or not.

If you can answer "YES" to the following seven questions, you probably have a solid foundation for de-escalation:

Can it be resolved peacefully?
Do you have an exit strategy?
Do you have a communication strategy?
Do you have at least one more person with you?
Are you capable of remaining solution-based?
Can you manage or avoid the audience?
Have the police been notified?

If you cannot answer yes to the seven triage questions, an exit strategy becomes a priority. You might not have the opportunity to exit at once; however, a hasty departure should be cued up; a quiet decision at the forefront of your mind. Once engaged in de-escalation we should pay close attention to the ABCs, three environments or indicators of increased risk:

A. Listen for outside influences: Agitated bystanders, sympathetic co-workers, and any other force counterproductive to de-escalation.

B. Continuous self-check: Your posture (does it represent a desire for a resolution or a defeated victim?). And volume (you and the agitated one), and other non-verbal clues (your projection and new clues related to the agitated one).

C. Pre-attack indicators: These may include direct threats, breaking items, and target glance. An increase in pre-attack indicators also leads to an exit strategy. Pre-attack indicators are deal-breakers; you are not bound to continue with de-escalation.

Deal-breakers encourage us to find a dignified exit or switch gears, "I want to talk with you, but not like this," or "Why don't we take a break, I certainly need one. I suggest we cool off and meet again later."

De-escalation:

1. Avoid harsh replies and don't continuously reiterate your point of view if it opposes the offender. De-escalation and the fight to be right cannot co-exist.

2. Know what upsets you; de-escalation involves a transfer of power; if you stay calm and reasonable, the offender will often do the same.

3. Practice the Platinum Rule! The Golden Rule encourages us to treat others as we prefer. The Platinum Rule of De-Escalation suggests we treat the offender as he would prefer; not soft submission; it is a de-escalation tactic, and it is never about you.

4. Decide to agree in general to universal pains, while reframing comments creating disagreement. If the offender's opinion is the world sucks, we can agree, it often does. If he says the government is evil, we can agree, some governments include unqualified people, and people are flawed. If he says he hates the boss and wants to kill her, we don't agree and shift to the emotion at hand. You might say "I understand you are angry and that must be painful." If he says his co-worker is a snitch and needs to die, we don't agree and shift to the greater emotion or feelings of betrayal. You might say "I too have felt

burned by an old friend. It was unpleasant until we worked it out. I can probably help with that."

5. Avoid statements and stick with questions. What can I do? If you could ask for any solution, what would that be? If you were in charge, what would you do to resolve this situation? I will be talking to those who can help, what would you like me to say? If you and I were on the same team, what would you want me to do (forced-teaming without the force.)?

6. Agree with empathy, not sympathy. Sympathy divides and creates distance as you elevate yourself by showing pity rather than understanding the circumstances. Understanding closes the emotional gap as you acknowledge the pain and the possible impact.

7. Be respectful of circumstances and the burden but avoid respecting or condoning the irrational behavior. My personal favorite, "I respect the pressure you're under, I've been under a lot of stress myself. It's not too late to handle it differently. Would you like to hear a few suggestions?"

8. Remember, any form of communication is better than none.

9. If the offender is mentally ill or delusional, avoid agreeing or affirming hallucinations or unrealistic conspiracies. Finding common ground is essential, but we should align ourselves without lying. Many years ago, I responded to a barricaded offender who had fired several rounds from his front and rear porch. The 17-hour negotiation involved hallucinations, which included combat boots surrounding his home. No people, just the boots. He asked several times, "Do you see them? You must be able to see them. Do you?" I responded respectfully, "No. I've looked, but I can't see anything like that. Am I missing something?" His response caught us off-guard. "I was testing you. I know you can't f***ing see them, people never understand what I see. At least you're not a f***ing liar." He surrendered without another shot fired, with no injuries, and he received treatment rather

than criminal charges. Even when the offender is mentally disturbed, he often understands those around him are not.

End of Chapter Eight

NOTES:

CHAPTER NINE

The Active Shooter

Of the many challenges in risk reduction, weighing our dramatic sensation against facts is paramount. Some colleagues prefer a statistical story, which motivates others at a level equal to watching paint dry. Other professional clients and students prefer the formal presentation; testimony straight from the mouth of a witness or the final paper from OSHA, the NTSB or the FBI. Many enjoy stories; one of America's favs and a training approach that consumes precious time; twice the time, to be exact, and why my presentations usually exceed the time allowed. I love stories; they fuel strong, persuasive, and lasting lessons. This chapter will side-step the eloquent narrative and the drama to drill down on what we know or think we know about the Active Shooter.

We don't have the numbers needed for a clear portrait; average facts about this offender don't exist, just early and anecdotal advice about an enigma. In the world of predictable harm, this offender has received recent attention; however, while a sketch exists, he still is a mystery. Getting inside the head and cold heart of the active shooter has been difficult, a curious dilemma hinting we may be looking at the symptom rather than the problem.

This chapter relies on research completed by my friends in

Quantico, Virginia; those in the Behavioral Science Unit of the FBI, the best in extracting the habits, styles, rage-points and other components of the offender. With a bias toward the active shooter, a comparatively rare offender, we'll extract significant facts compiled in 2017. I've selected items fitting a real-world need, and clues that capture 'Deviations from the Norm;' respecting Dimension #1 from the five components of predictable harm. The patterns of the most destructive and violent offenders may lead to a reality check or dispel a few popular myths; valuable knowledge based on verified facts.

Friends and professional peers have asked why I don't dedicate more time to the 'Active-Shooter' and less on 'low-level' assaults, accidents, injuries at home, and other on-the-job casualties. I did some soul-searching leading to a partial answer, which includes two questions to consider:

1. Where or what are the risks of harm to you, a professional colleague or a loved one?

2. Is the active shooter a primary concern or is the higher risk found in 'low-level' assault or accidents?

Many studies and academic papers refer to low-level accidents, minor assaults, and the day-to-day cases that get little media or mention by statisticians and organizations who master the count. The Active Shooter fits our Hollywood Mentality, even though he rarely compares to the high number of casualties in the low visibility category. That said, he's still a trendsetter, a terrorist, and a killer worthy of our examination.

Before we dive into the Active-Shooter, we need to compare his destruction to some of the frequent assaults and injuries rarely hitting the media. I believe 'low-level' assaults and 'routine' injuries, as reported, have been labeled as such by those never suffering a 'low-level' fracture or 'routine' kick to the groin. Those pontificating the minor nature of assault and injury, have probably missed out on the

No Further Harm: A Purely Predictable Path

broken nose, shattered dental work, and that crushed eye socket; all labeled small in a media industry suffering the addiction of more dramatic needs. They likely avoided that 'petty' street robbery, leaving a woman unconscious with a 'low-level' concussion, and they have never been bothered by a 'minor' fall at a construction site, with or without the 'low-level' body piercing via rebar. Excuse my sarcasm, but there is rarely a minor casualty; those qualifying these cases as insignificant have disconnected from the reality of danger, pain, and the trauma. They may not know anyone with tough history, have not been victimized, or can't relate to the trauma they don't understand.

If you have been in the crosshairs of an offender or injured on the job, the ugliness is anything but low-level, never minor, the trip to the Emergency Room rarely routine. Published government reports are not suggesting these daily incidents are minor. The truth is the frequency of these high-volume events numb the media coverage; as a reporter once told me, 'Dog Bites Man' is a dull, low-level headline. But a man biting a dog will probably make the news. The public, some federal agencies, and media are naturally drawn to the drama like moths to a flame. Only those cases of significant trauma or unusual details, intentions, and bizarre accidents survive the editors cutting tool.

Active Shooter cases, as horrible as they are, are not the probable cause of death in North America, Europe, and the UK, but they meet or exceed the threshold for terror, shock, and a news story. The active-shooter also helps us understand predictable versus random violence; common mistakes leading to serious harm, and the potentially life-ending violence we hope to avoid. Today's 'low-level' stuff and the near-miss still deserve our focus as they become tomorrow's fatalities. That said, details exposed in mass violence, to include the active-shooter, also deserve a closer look as they affirm lessons we can no longer deny.

The active shooter is an enigma; his uncontrolled rage, lack of consistency, and his unpredictable internal flash-fire are off-the-chart. Most disturbing but helpful, the active shooter often displays anger long before the morbid mass-killing; the deep-seated rage-pattern of the active-shooter is nearly identical to an angry employee or friend who recently hit the radar screen as a potential problem.

The cycle of rage announces itself early in life. Unchecked, the cycle continues, accelerates, and spins out of control: Tantrums move to a more severe case of throwing objects; breaking objects graduate to verbal or written threats of harm; unchecked, shoving becomes the foreplay to a wild punch, kick, and a felony aggravated assault, eventually devolving to committing a murder. The active shooter has graduated to a level of extreme violence as his answer, usually after a continuum of dynamic events have failed. He's difficult to understand, but his acts are often predictable.

I frame every violent offender as a man after solutions; failing in every forceful attempt only to double-down and try again. For a myriad of reasons and much like an addict, he rejects all guidance related to the core problem. The addict often blames everything but the drug, and the active shooter blames everyone but himself. The history of the active shooter often includes changing and blaming everything except his use of violence. It is difficult to grasp but statistically supported, today's active-shooter was yesterday's possible anger problem.

The Las Vegas Sniper unleashed his rage in October 2017, killing nearly 60 innocent victims; however, he was a man known for habitually losing his temper by July 2014. Charles Whitman, the sniper behind the 'Clock Tower' brand and fame, was not an exception to the rule. A 25-year-old architectural engineering student, Whitman was one of the first Active Shooters. The disturbed military vet perched himself in the campus clock tower (University of

Texas, Austin). Whitman wounded 28 and killed 17 on August 1, 1966. Was it predictable? I don't know, but history supplies a clue. By January 1964 he had set up a reputation for blowing up after a beer and a simple disagreement.

The pattern is known; ignore the rage pattern and it escalates. When we address the early outbursts, the evidence of inappropriate anger, it often de-escalates. As part of a training triage, I often ask clients, 'If you had to, could you provide the name of the employee or student likely to blow a fuse or become enraged during a standard verbal disagreement?' Every client, 100% of the leaders who run a company of 300 or more said yes, they could name him. Teachers serving a student base of 700 or more, also say they can name a ticking timebomb disguised as a student. Business leaders and educators have predicted, via the short-list, who will be behind the next act of violence. Workplace and school violence offer an extreme example of rage. The highest level of destructive behavior includes predictable clues and rage-based tendencies; evidence presented long-before the actual force. In many cases, leaders say they can't do anything about the rage-based player. I interpret that to mean they prefer not to do anything or don't know what to do.

Our study of the active shooter is essential; however, a focus on our behavior and the actions of those closest to us is likely to save more lives. Missed cues, clues, our fear of communicating observations, severe warning signs ignored, and a subculture of denial - these are the behaviors, our behavior, days and weeks before the shooting starts. Prediction works! Start the conversation early as the gap between general anger and a murderous rage is often difficult to detect.

Examine the Active Shooter Separately

I most appreciate reports that confirm the numbers and allow stakeholders, like you and me, to draw our conclusions. In nearly every public gathering discussing risk, injury, and fatality, someone will approach me and compare their hazardous line-of-work to workplace violence. The side-by-side examination usually starts with "Yeah, but more people die in deep-sea fishing accidents ...jogging ...skydiving ... than school shootings." Statistically speaking, they are correct. The small number argument prompts debate and makes sense until we add three words: Assumption of Risk. The fact is most on the job incidents, and accidents occur within the historical confines of known-risk or the assumption of risk. The Active

Shooter forces his rage and intentional harm in the environment where we least expect it. Evil acts of the Active Shooter direct violence at those merely taking a needed break from stress. Innocent people enter the church, schoolyard, and the movie theater under the assumption of safety. The Active Shooter has stolen that peaceful assumption, and he's a part of the domestic terrorism threat.

It appears the details surrounding the Active Shooter call for more study and a new strategy. He has exceeded causation reports or white papers covering the standard crook. The rest of this section captures incidents from 2014 - 2017, and the most recent 12 Month Total Count. Stats are limited to the USA for a good reason. While Kamikaze Pilots originated in Japan, and Suicide Bombers are usually connected to the Middle East, the USA acknowledges the unique stylistic claim for the Active Shooter. Active-Shooter Cases include 30 acts in 2017, the highest on record.

Right-Sizing the Active Shooter

According to OSHA, 4,821 U.S. workers have died on the job in one year. A sizable percentage of these fatalities involve the construction industry, resulting from many hazards that exist on construction sites. Leading workplace deaths, called the "Fatal Four," include:

1. Falls: Roughly 36.5% of all deaths in the workplace occurred due to employees falling. Falls also top the list in home injuries, the only injury sharing the top spot. The injury leading to death includes workers who have fallen off ladders, stumbled and rolled from roofs, scaffolding, large skyscraper construction areas, etc.

2. Struck by an Object: An estimated 10.1% of deaths occurred due to items under crane hook, falling product, and tools, or objects stored or positioned improperly.

3. Electrocutions: About 8.6% of employees died due to electrocution. Electrocution resulted from exposed wiring, wet conditions while outlets are exposed, etc.

4. Pinch-point, Caught-in or Caught-between: Employees caught in or between machines, devices, or tools accounted for about 2.5% of deaths.

The reports do not mention the unfortunate reality, which is tough to measure, and most difficult to discuss. Before the fall, preceding the electrocution, before getting struck by debris, and just before the reality of being crushed in a pinch-point, we find a contributing factor. I am not minimizing the tragic results of construction accidents; the women and men deserve the utmost respect for their challenging work in a dangerous occupation. The fact remains construction accidents occur within the confines of known-risk or the assumption of risk. The active shooter forces intentional harm in the environment of low-to-no expectation of danger.

The construction fatal-four includes the unspoken social contract of assumed risk; employees suit up, sign in, gear up, and understand the inherent danger of the work. Policing, firefighting, marathon running, waste management, and house painting include a level of assumed risk. Fall protection fails, exposed wiring went unnoticed, unsecured loads fail, and a short-cut ends it all. Distilled to the lowest common denominator, human factors in the environment of assumed risk kill. Distractions, fatigue, inadequate training, erosion of policy, safety compliance, predictably worn-out equipment end lives. Our failure to inspect, attending to multiple projects in one pay period, and preoccupation share the top billing in causes. In the final analysis and reducing the problem to the lowest common denominator, everything bent, broken or killed under the umbrella of on the job, is a human cause.

Initially, construction and other work-related deaths in high-risk categories appear to present wildly different victimology or predictable risk. Once compared to an active shooter case, and a lengthy list of other accidents and intentional acts, we find common themes in the five dimensions of predictable harm. In nearly every case, there is an Environmental Norm (1) before the accident or the first shot fired. The norm changes before the casualty. We find External Clues (2) presented and missed, and Internal Cues (3) within more than one peer, witness, or co-worker (intuition or gut-level red flags) noticed or cued-up prior to harm but not discussed. Critical Solo or Stand-Alone Cues and Clues (4) were usually present before the death, often within moments or minutes of damage. And finally, we find a hazard we could have reduced by Shared Risk or Rapid Communication (5); information, caution, and changes we could have or should have communicated and didn't. The error is usually not intentional, one or more of the five dimensions of predictable harm missed without malice.

Those killed by an active shooter are usually congregating under no assumption of risk. The shock, innocence, and age of the victims make these cases deeply disturbing. In 2017 there were 30 separate active shootings in the United States, the most considerable number 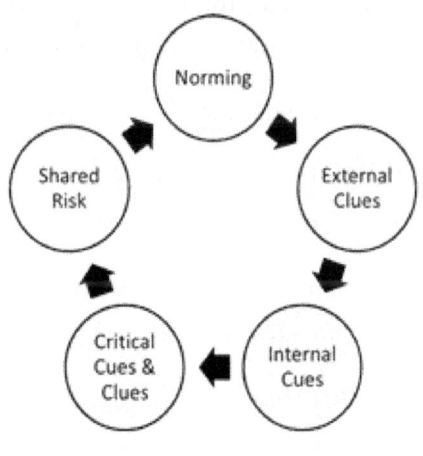 ever recorded for one year. The contagion of fear combined with the politics of protection make these cases high-stress and disempowering. Most troublesome is the belief there is nothing we can do to prevent a mass shooting. This is simply false. True, we avoid discussing the available forecast, but clues and cues are normally available.

We can do something; people don't just snap, they are predictable, and we have many examples of the shooter who planned and never completed a mass shooting. The latter holds our solution; the habits, the haunts, and the vulnerability of shooters who tipped their cards and lost the opportunity to play out their violent scheme. We have much to do that we are not doing in the predictable world of the somewhat new active shooter. Over 50% of the mass-homicides hold lessons as simple as those found on the Cruise Ship Costa Concordia. Rules we know but may not follow, and warnings we see or feel but may not share.

Portrait of the Active Shooter:

Over 63 active shooters were studied in the most recent research, authored by the FBI Behavioral Science Unit, Quantico, Virginia. There were very few patterns or trends (aside from gender), reinforcing the concept that there is no one "profile" of an active shooter, elevating the difficulty in forecasting violence. One-half of the mass homicides could have prevented. Here's what we know:

1. 77% of the shooters spend a week or longer planning their attack.

2. 46% need more than a week to obtain the means, equipment, and weaponry for an assault.

3. Most active shooters obtained their firearms legally, with only small percentages obtaining a gun illegally.

4. The FBI could verify 25% of active shooters previously diagnosed with mental illness. Of those examined, only three previously diagnosed with a psychotic disorder. Legally speaking, 60 active shooters were considered sane in the days, weeks, and months preceding the assault and homicide.

5. Active shooters were typically experiencing multiple stressors in the year before they attacked.

6. On average, each active shooter displayed 4 to 5 concerning behaviors observable to others around the shooter (External Clues and Solo or Stand-Alone Clues) before the shooting. The most often occurring behaviors were related to the active shooter's mental health, problematic interpersonal interactions, and communication reaching or exceeding violent intent (threats).

7. For active shooters under age 18, school peers and teachers were more likely to see behaviors than family members. For active shooters 18 years old and over, spouses/domestic partners were the most likely to perceive the indicators or behaviors.

8. When concerning behavior was seen by others, the most common response was to communicate directly to the active shooter (83%) or do nothing (54%). Just because concerning behavior was recognized does not necessarily mean that it was reported to law enforcement.

9. In those cases where the active shooter's primary grievance is named, common complaints related to an adverse interpersonal or employment action against the shooter (49%).

10. In most cases (64%) at least one of the victims was explicitly targeted by the active shooter.

Methodology:

With the goal of carefully reviewing the pre-attack lives and behaviors of the active shooters, the FBI developed a unique protocol of 104 variables covering, among other things:

- **Planning and preparation**
- **Acquisition of firearms related to the attack**
- **Stressors**
- **Grievance formation**
- **Concerning pre-attack behaviors and communications**
- **Targeting decisions**
- **Mental health**

Given the subtle nature of many of the factors relevant to the inquiry, the FBI decided to use data that have been verified to the highest possible extent, relying almost exclusively on information contained in official law enforcement investigative files. For this reason, this report includes only those cases where the FBI obtained law enforcement investigative files that had "background" materials (e.g., interviews with family members, acquaintances, neighbors; school or employment records; writings generated by the subject) adequate to answer the protocol questions. Also, this report focused on naming pre-attack behaviors of those on a trajectory to violence, active shooting events which appeared to be spontaneous reactions to situational factors (e.g., fights that escalated) excluded, resulting in a final sample of 63 active shooting incidents.

The use of law enforcement investigative case files as the primary source of data makes this study unique in comparison to other reports that typically rely upon unverified data derived from open sources. The comprehensive evaluation of law enforcement case files for suitability and completeness also contributed to the substantial time it has taken to prepare and publish this study. Refined data included the following characteristics:

■ Events end before law enforcement arrived;
■ More likely to occur in an educational facility or a house of worship; and
■ Were more likely to stop with the active shooter committing suicide.

The study relied on a three-stage coding process; first, two researchers read all case materials and independently coded each of the cases. The researchers took a conservative approach, declining to definitively answer any question that was not supported by the record or specific evidence. Second, another experienced coder (the "reviewer") also read each investigative file. In the final stage, the coders and the reviewer met for each of the 63 cases, compared answers, discussed disagreements, and produced a single reconciled set of data.

Shooter Demographics:

The sample included individuals who varied widely along a range of demographic factors making it impossible to create a demographic profile of an active shooter. Indeed, the findings and conclusions of this study considering the reality that these 63 active shooters did not appear to be consistent in any way; not found before the attack based on demographics alone.

Age: The youngest active shooter was 12 years old, and the oldest was 88 years old with an average age of 37.8 years. 7 Active shooters were under the age of 18.

Gender: The sample was overwhelmingly male (94%), with only four females in the data set (6%).

Highest Level of Education: None of the active shooters under the age of 18 had completed high school, and one (age 12) had not yet entered high school. When known, the highest level of education of adults varied considerably.

Employment: The 7 active shooters who were under 18 years old were all students. Nearly equal percentages of the adult active shooters 18 years or older were employed as were unemployed and retired or disabled with and without benefits.

Military: Of the active shooters 18 and older, 24% had at least some military experience, with six having served in the Army, three in the Marines, two in the Navy, and one each in the Air Force and the Coast Guard.

Relationship Status: The active shooters were mostly single at the time of the offense (57%). Thirteen percent were married, while another 13% were divorced. The remaining 11% were either partnered but not married or separated.

Criminal Convictions and Anti-Social Behavior:

Nineteen of the active shooters aged 18 and over (35%) had adult convictions before the active shooting event. The study does not include juvenile adjudications; therefore, we did not run the analyses on those aged 17 and younger. In sum, the active shooters had a limited history of adult convictions for violent crime and a limited history of adult convictions of any kind.

We found evidence that 62% of the active shooters had a history of acting in an abusive, harassing, or oppressive way (e.g., excessive workplace intimidation); 16% had engaged in domestic or intimate partner violence, and 11% had been involved in a stalking-related offense or conduct. The stalking data may be underrepresented given the high percentage of unknown responses as related to stalking behaviors (68%).

Planning and Preparation:

This dimension of the study examined two related but separate temporal aspects of the active shooters' pre-attack lives — total time spent planning the attack and the entire time spent preparing for the attack. The purpose of analyzing these chronologies was to set up the broad parameters during which active shooters were moving toward the attack.

Planning:

In this context, the plan means the full range of considerations involved in carrying out a shooting attack and includes the decision to engage in violence, selecting specific or random targets, conducting surveillance, and addressing all ancillary practical issues such as victim schedules, transportation, and site access. Planning is more specific than a general intent to act violently and involves the thought processes necessary to bring about an intended outcome. Since planning is primarily an internal thought process, it was often difficult to find objective, observable indications of an active shooter's planning. In nearly half of the cases, the total time spent planning is unknown. However, this is different than declaring that there was no evidence of planning at all because in every case there was at least some evidence that the active shooter planned the attack; the challenge was learning when the planning began.

In setting up the total duration of planning, the FBI looked for evidence of behaviors that were observable (e.g., conversations, conducting surveillance) as well as in materials that were private to the active shooter (e.g., journals, computer hard drives) and likely unknowable to others until after the attack. There was a wide range of planning duration in the 34 cases where time could be determined.

Regarding specific planning, care in the interpretation of the data is essential. For instance, our study shows that few active shooters overall approached or conducted surveillance on their target (14%), and fewer still researched or studied the target site where the attack occurred (10%). While this could say that the active shooters were uninterested in knowing about their targets or attack sites in advance or engaged in little tactical planning, this is inconsistent with the operational experience of the FBI.

The likely reason for this finding is that the active shooters often attacked people and places with which they were already familiar. There was a known connection between the active shooters and the attack site in most cases (73%). Often a workplace or former workplace for those 18 and older (35%), and almost always a school or former school for those younger than 18 (88%), showing that in most cases the active shooter was already familiar with the attack site and persons located at the site.

Preparing:

Preparation narrowly defined for this story; actions taken to get the means for the attack, typically items such as a handgun or rifle, ammunition, unique clothing or body armor. The focus was on activities that could have been noticed by others (e.g., a visit to a gun store, the delivery of ammunition) and which were essential to the execution of the plan. The FBI was able to find evidence of time spent preparing in more cases than for time spent planning (likely reflecting the open nature of getting materials as opposed to the presumably mostly internal thought process of planning). In more than half of the cases where the time spent preparing was known, active shooters spent one week or less preparing for the attack.

As part of the review of the active shooter's preparations, the FBI explored investigative records and tried to show how each active shooter obtained the firearm(s) used during the attack. Most commonly (40%), the active shooter bought a firearm or firearms legally and correctly to perpetrate the attack. A small percentage obtained guns illegally (2%) or stole the gun (6%). Some (11%) borrowed or took the firearm from a person known

to them. A considerable number of active shooters (35%) already owned a firearm and did not appear (based on longevity of possession) to have obtained it for the express purpose of committing the shooting.

Active shooters generally take some time to plan and carry out the attack. However, retrospectively determining the exact moment when an active shooter decided to engage in violence is a

challenging and imprecise process. In reviewing indicators of planning and preparing, the FBI notes that most active shooters (who showed evidence of these processes in an obvious manner) spent days, weeks, and sometimes months getting ready to attack. In fact, in those cases where it could be determined, 77% of the active shooters spent a week or longer planning their attack, and 46% spent a week or longer preparing.

Stress and the Active Shooter:

Stressors are physical, psychological, or social forces that place real or perceived demands/pressures on an individual and which may cause mental or physical distress. Stress is a well-established correlate of criminal behavior. For this study, a wide variety of potential stressors were assessed, including financial pressures, physical health concerns, interpersonal conflicts with family, friends, and colleagues (work or school), mental health issues, criminal and civil law issues, and substance abuse.

The FBI recognizes that most (if not all) people in some way confront similar issues regularly in their daily lives and that most have adequate personal resources, psychological resiliency, and coping skills to navigate such challenges without resorting to violence successfully. Therefore, the FBI focused on naming stressors that appeared to have more than a minimal amount of adverse impact on that individual, and which were sufficiently significant to have been memorialized, shared, or otherwise noted in some way (e.g., in the active shooter's own writings, in conversation with family or friends, work files, court records). Given the fluid nature of some (although not all) of the stressors, the analysis limited to the year preceding the attack.

The variables treated as binary, that is, either the stressor was present or not, without regard for the number of separate circumstances giving rise to stress. So, an active shooter who had a conflict with one family member and a gunman who had disputes with several family members were both coded as "yes" for "conflict with other family members." Overall, the data reflects that active shooters were typically experiencing multiple stressors (an average of 3.6 separate stressors) in the year before they attacked. For example, in the year before his attack, one active shooter was facing disciplinary action at school for abuse of a teacher, was himself abused and neglected at home, and had a significant conflict with his peers. Another active shooter was under six separate stressors, including a recent arrest for drunk driving, accumulating significant debt, facing eviction, showing signs of both depression and anxiety, and experiencing both the criminal and civil law repercussions of an incident three months before the attack where he barricaded himself in a hotel room, and the police called.

The only stressor that applied to more than half the sample was mental health (62%). Other stressors that were present in at least 20% of the sample were related to financial strain, employment, conflicts with friends and peers, marital problems, drug, and alcohol abuse, other, conflict at school, and physical injury.

Table of Stressors:

Mental health 62%
Financial strain 49%
Job-related 35%
Conflicts with friends/peers 29%
Marital problems 27%
Abuse of illicit drugs/alcohol 22%
Other (e.g. caregiving responsibilities) 14%
Conflict at school 22%
Physical injury 21%
Conflict with parents 18%
Conflict with other family members 16%
Sexual stress/frustration 13%
Criminal problems 11%
Death of friend/relative 6%
None 2%

Mental Health Issues of the Active Shooter:

There are significant and complex considerations on mental health, both because it is the most common stressor and because of the common but mistaken inclination to assume that anyone who commits an actual shooting must de facto be mentally ill. First, "mental health" is not synonymous with a diagnosis of mental illness. The stressor "mental health" says that the active shooter appeared to be struggling with (most commonly) depression, anxiety, paranoia, etc. in their daily life in the year before the attack.

There may be complex interactions with other stressors that give rise to what may ultimately be transient manifestations of behaviors and moods that would not be enough to call for a formal diagnosis of mental illness.

In this context, it is exceedingly important to highlight that the FBI could only verify that 25% (total of 16) of the active shooters were known to have been diagnosed by a mental health professional with a mental illness of any kind before offense. The FBI could not determine if a diagnosis existed in 37% (23) of cases. Of the 16 cases with a diagnosis, before the incident could be learned, 12 active shooters had a mood disorder; four were diagnosed with an anxiety disorder; three were diagnosed with a psychotic disorder, and two were diagnosed with a personality disorder. Having a diagnosed mental illness was unsurprisingly related to a higher incidence of concurrent mental health stressors among active shooters.

Most active shooters experienced multiple stressors in their lives before the attack. While the FBI did not measure the active shooters' reactions to stressors, what appears to be noteworthy and of importance to threat assessment professionals is the active shooters' ability to navigate conflict and resiliency (or lack thereof) in the face of challenges. Given the high prevalence of financial and job-related stressors as well as conflict with peers and partners, those in contact with a person of concern at his/her place of employment may have unique insights to inform a threat assessment.

Considering the extremely high lifetime prevalence of the symptoms of mental illness among the U.S. population, formally diagnosed mental illness is not a specific predictor of violence of any type, let alone targeted violence. Absent concrete evidence, careful consideration should be given to social and contextual factors that might interact with any mental health issue before concluding that an active shooting was "caused" by mental illness. In short, declarations that all active shooters must be mentally ill are misleading.

Concerning Behaviors of the Active Shooter:

Concerning behaviors are observable behaviors exhibited by the active shooter. For this study, a wide variety of concerning behaviors were considered, including those related to potential symptoms of a mental health disorder, interpersonal interactions, quality of the active shooter's thinking or communication, recklessness, violent media usage, changes in hygiene and weight, impulsivity, firearm behavior, and physical aggression. Although these may be related to stressors in the active shooter's life, the focus here was not on the internal, subjective experience. The number of documented, diagnosed mental illness may be the result of several factors, including those related to situational factors (access to health care) as well as those related to the study factors (access to mental health records).

While the assessment of stressors is meant to supply insight into the active shooter's inner turmoil, the examination of concerning behaviors addresses a related but separate issue — the possibility of finding active shooters before they attack by being alert for observable, concerning behaviors. The FBI looked for documented confirmation that someone noticed a facet of the shooter's behavior causing the person to feel a "more than minimal" degree of unease about the well-being and safety of those around the active shooter.

Before examining what behaviors were observable by others, it is useful to address the widespread belief that active shooters tend to be cut off from those around them. In general, the active shooters in were not completely isolated and had at least some social connection to another person.

While most of the active shooters age 18 and older were single/never married (51%) or separated/divorced (22%) at the time of the attack, the majority did live with someone else (68%). Most had significant in-person social interactions with at least one other person in the year before the attack (86%), and more than a quarter of them had substantial online interactions with another person within a year of the attack (27%). All active shooters either: a) lived with someone, or b) had significant in-person or online social interactions

Since the observation of concerning behaviors offers the opportunity for intervention before the attack, this study examines not only what was observed, but when the observations were made, who made them, and what if anything the person(s) did about these observations. To better serve threat assessment teams, mental health professionals, community resources, and law enforcement officials, the FBI expanded the inquiry to capture behaviors that may have been observed at any point (in many cases beyond one year) before the attack.

Overall, active shooters showed concerning behaviors in multiple ways, with an average of 4.7 concerning behaviors per active shooter. Behaviors observed in more than half of the sample were related to the shooter's mental health, interpersonal interactions, leakage (the communication to a third-party of an intent to harm someone, discussed with threats in a separate section), and the quality of the active shooter's thinking or communication.

Inappropriate firearms behavior was noted in approximately one fifth of the active shooters, while drug and alcohol abuse figured even less prominently in the sample. For purpose of the study, contextually inappropriate firearms behavior is defined as an interest in or use of firearms that appeared unusual given the active shooter's background and experience with firearms.

Breakdown of Concerning Behaviors:

Mental health 62%
Interpersonal interactions 57%
Leakage (shared intentions) 56%
Quality of thinking or communication 54%
Work performance 46%
School performance 42%
Threats/confrontations 35%
Anger 33%
Physical aggression 33%
Risk-taking 21%
Firearm behavior 21%
Violent media usage 19%
Weight/eating 13%
Drug abuse 13%
Impulsivity 11%
Alcohol abuse 10%
Physical health 10%
Other (e.g. idolizing criminals) 8%
Sexual behavior 6%
Quality of sleep 5%
Hygiene/appearance 3%

When Concerning Behaviors Noticed?
(Deviation from the Environmental Norm):

Since most active shooters (all but three) displayed at least two concerning behaviors, there are several separate ways to assess the data. One way is to examine the data by an active shooter and to see the first instance that any concerning behavior was noticed (this could not be determined for three active shooters). Figure 9 shows this data and helps frame the longest time before a shooting during which others were concerned about the active shooter's behavior.

Again, this chart shows the first instance of any concerning behavior, and it should be kept in mind that this behavior might not have been the type that by itself would cause a reasonable person to be alarmed or to report it to others. For example, a co-worker who noticed that an active shooter had more than the normal amount of conflict with a supervisor might be unlikely to take any action.

Perhaps only after an attack and with the benefit of hindsight would this singular behavior be — in and of itself — troubling or concerning. Yet, on average, each active shooter displayed four to five concerning behaviors over time. While it may only be the interaction and cumulative effect of these behaviors that would cause alarm, early recognition, and detection of growing or interrelated problems may help to mitigate the potential for violence.

In What Way Were the Concerning Behaviors Noticed?

Concerning behaviors came to the attention to others in a variety of ways, with some far more common than others. The most common way in which concerning behaviors were noticed was verbal communication by the active shooter (95%), followed by seeing the physical actions of the active shooter (86%), written communication (27%), and finally, instances where concerning behavior was displayed online (16%). A vast majority of active shooters (89%) showed concerning behaviors that noticed in multiple ways.

Who Noticed the Concerning Behaviors?

At least one person noticed a concerning behavior in every active shooter's life, and on average, people from three diverse groups noticed concerning behaviors for each active shooter. As shown below, classmates (for those who were students), partners (for those in relationships), family members and friends most often noticed concerning behavior, followed by co-workers, other, and law enforcement:

Schoolmate* 92%

Spouse/domestic partner** 87%
Teacher/school staff 75%
Family member 68%
Friend 51%
Co-worker 40%
Other (e.g., neighbors) 37%
Law enforcement 25%
Online individual 10%
Religious mentor 5%

* Percentage calculated only with those active shooters who were students at the time of the offense ** Percentage calculated only with those active shooters who were in a relationship at the time of the offense.

What, If Anything, Did the Concerned Party Do?

If the person recognizes behaviors as problematic but takes no action, the opportunity for intervention is missed. Whether and how a person responds to an active shooter's concerning a host of personal and situational likely influences behavior factors (e.g., whether the behavior is threatening to the observer or others, the relationship of the observer and active shooter, avenues for anonymous reporting, and/or confidence in authorities or others to address the behavior).

In this study, even in cases where an active shooter displayed a variety of concerning behaviors that might say an intent to act violently, the observer(s) of that information did not necessarily pass it along to anyone else. As shown above, the people most likely to notice concerning behaviors were those who knew the active shooter best — family, friends, and classmates. For the very reason, they are the people most likely to take note of concerning behaviors; they are also people who may feel constrained from acting on these concerns because of loyalty, disbelief, or fear of the consequences.

Active shooters displayed multiple concerning behaviors and in most cases, others saw these behaviors. The most common response was to communicate directly to the active shooter (83%) or do nothing (54%). Thus, in many instances, concern stayed between the person who noticed the behavior and the active shooter. The next most common responses were report the active shooter to a non-law enforcement authority (51%); discuss the concerning behavior with a friend or family member (49%); and, report the active shooter to law enforcement authority (41%).

The FBI is aware that in retrospect certain facts may take on a heightened degree of significance that may not have been clear at the time. Nevertheless, understanding that there are often opportunities before shooting to recognize behaviors that may suggest progression toward violence, the FBI is highlighting the most common behaviors displayed in the sample. There is no single warning sign, checklist, or algorithm for assessing behaviors that find a prospective active shooter. Instead, there appears to be a complex combination of behaviors and interactions with bystanders that may often occur in the days, weeks, and months leading up to an attack. Early recognition and reporting of concerning behaviors to law enforcement or threat assessment professionals may start significant opportunities for mitigation.

Primary Complaint or Grievance:

A grievance is defined for this study as the cause of the active shooter's distress or resentment; a feeling — not necessarily based in reality — of having been wronged or treated unfairly or inappropriately. More than a typical feeling of resentment or passing anger, a grievance often results in a grossly distorted preoccupation with a sense of injustice, like an injury that does not heal. These thoughts can saturate a person's thinking and foster a pervasive sense of imbalance between self-image and the (real or perceived) humiliation. This nagging sense of unfairness can spark an overwhelming desire to "right the wrong" and achieve a measure of satisfaction and/or revenge. In some cases, an active shooter might have what appeared to be multiple grievances but, where possible, the FBI looked to determine the primary grievance. Based on a review of the academic literature and the facts of the cases themselves, the FBI found eight categories of grievances, with an added category of "other" for grievances that were entirely idiosyncratic.

The FBI could not find a primary grievance for 13 (21%) of the active shooters because there was insufficient evidence to make that determination. While it may be particularly difficult to understand the motivation(s) for attacks that do not appear to be based on identifiable grievances, these active shooters still displayed concerning behaviors, were under identifiable stressors and engaged in planning and preparation activities. For example, for the active shooters where no grievance could be named, all had at least two behaviors (with an average of 5.4 behaviors) that were noted to be concerning by others.

The majority (79%) of the active shooters did appear to be acting in accord with a grievance of some kind. Of course, the grievance itself may not have been reasonable or even grounded, but it appeared to serve as the rationale for the eventual attack, giving a sense of purpose to the shooter. Most of these grievances seem to have originated in response to some specific action taken on the active shooter. Whether interpersonal, employment, governmental, academic, or financial, these actions were (or were perceived to be) directed against the active shooter personally. In contrast, grievances are driven by more global or broad considerations — such as ideology or hatred of a group — account for less than 7% of the overall cases. Active shooters harbored grievances that were distinctly personal to them and the circumstances of their daily lives.

Primary Grievance of the Active Shooter:

Adverse interpersonal action against the shooter 33%
Adverse employment action against the shooter 16%
Other (e.g. general hatred of others) 10%
Adverse governmental action against the shooter 5%
Adverse academic action against the shooter 3%
Adverse financial action against the shooter 3%
Domestic 3%
Hate crime 3%
Ideology/extremism 3%
Unknown 21%

Precipitating Events:

Of the 50 active shooters who had an identifiable grievance, nearly half of them experienced a precipitating or triggering event related to the grievance (44%). Seven active shooters (14%) did not experience a precipitating event, and the FBI could not determine whether the remaining 21 (42%) did. Precipitating events generally occurred close in time to the shooting and included circumstances such as an adverse ruling in a legal matter, romantic rejection, and the loss of a job. These precipitating events were of more consequence in the timing of the attack, and while they appear to have accelerated the active shooter's movement on the trajectory to violence, they did not by themselves appear to set the course.

Note: Many people have grievances and never act violently. What caused the active shooters in this study to act the way they did cannot be explained simply by the presence of a grievance. There was likely the interaction of a variety of operational considerations and psychological stressors that eventually crystallized in the decision to ignore non-violent options and choose to attack. However, the types of grievances most commonly experienced by the active shooters in this study may be important considerations for the many threat assessment teams and law enforcement professionals who work each day to assess a subject's progression along the pathway to violence.

Concerning Communications (Threats and Leakage):

Threats:

One useful way to analyze concerns in communications is to divide them into two categories: threats/confrontations and leakage of intent.

Threats are direct communications to a target of intent to harm and may be delivered in person or by other means (e.g., text, email, telephone). For this study, threats need not be verbalized or written; the FBI considered in-person confrontations that were intended to intimidate or cause safety concerns for the target as falling under the category of threats as well.

More than half of the 40 active shooters who had a target made threats or had a prior confrontation (55%). When threats or confrontations occurred, they were almost always in person (95%) and only infrequently in writing or electronically (14%). Two active shooters made threats both in person and in writing/electronically.

Leakage: Another Word for Clues:

Leakage occurs when a person intentionally or unintentionally reveals clues to a third-party about feelings, thoughts, fantasies, attitudes or intentions that may signal the intent to commit a violent act. Indirect threats of harm are included as leakage, but so are less obvious, subtle threats, innuendo about a desire to commit a violent attack, or boasts about the ability to harm others. Leakage can be found not only in verbal communications but also in writings (e.g., journals, school assignments, artwork, poetry) and online interactions (e.g., blogs, tweets, texts, video postings).

Prior research has shown that leakage of intent to commit violence is common before attacks perpetrated by both adolescents and adults but are more common among adolescents. Here, too, leakage was prevalent, with over half of the active shooters leaking intent to commit violence (56%). 88% of those active shooters age 17 and younger leaked intent to commit violence, while 51% of active adult shooters leaked their intent. The leaked intent to commit violence was not always directed at the eventual victims of the shootings; in some cases what was communicated was a more general goal of doing harm to others, apparently without a person or group in mind. For example, one active shooter talked to a clerk at a gas station about killing "a family" and another expressed interest in becoming a sniper like a

character featured in The Turner Diaries. In 16 of the 40 cases (40%) where the active shooter had a target, however, the leaked intent to act violently was directly on that target. In these cases, the leakage was generally a statement to a third-party of the intent to specifically harm the target.

Legacy Tokens: Communication Clues:

Finally, the FBI considered whether an active shooter had constructed a "legacy token" which has been defined as a communication prepared by the offender to claim credit for the attack and articulate the motives underlying the shooting. Examples of legacy tokens include manifestos, videos, social media postings, or other communications deliberately created by the shooter and delivered or staged for discovery by others, usually near in time to the shooting. In 30% of the cases included in this study, the active shooter created a legacy token prior to the attack.

It is important to highlight that most direct threats were verbally delivered by the offender to a future victim. Only a small percentage of threats were communicated via writing or electronically. In many ways, this is not surprising. Written threats against a target (e.g., "I'm going to shoot and kill everyone here on Tuesday") often spark a predictable response that includes a heightened law enforcement presence and the enhancement of security barriers. These responses are highly undesirable to an offender planning an active shooting. Verbal threats issued directly to another person appear to be far more common among the active shooters.

Limitations:

The findings presented in this report reflect a thorough and careful review of the data derived almost exclusively from law enforcement records. Nevertheless, there are limitations to the study which should be kept in mind before drawing any conclusions based on the findings. This is a purely descriptive study. Except for mental health and suicidal behaviors, the FBI did not make any comparisons to the general population or to criminals who were not active shooters.

Active-Shooter Portrait Conclusion:

The ability to use case files (as compared to open-source documents) allowed the FBI to carefully examine both the internal issues experienced and the behaviors proved by active shooters in the weeks and months preceding their attacks. What appears is a complex and troubling picture of individuals who fail to successfully navigate multiple stressors in their lives while concurrently displaying four to five observables concerning behaviors, engaging in planning and preparation, and often communicating threats or leaking indications of an intent to attack. As an active shooter progresses on a trajectory towards violence, these observable behaviors may represent critical opportunities for detection and disruption.

The successful prevention of an active shooting often depends on the collective and collaborative engagement of varied community members: law enforcement officials, teachers, mental health care professionals, family members, threat assessment professionals, friends, social workers, school resource officer, and many others. A shared awareness of the common observable behaviors proven by the active shooters in this study may help to prompt inquiries at every stage of intervention.

End of Formal Active-Shooter Report

If you found the analysis of the Active-Shooter confusing or disturbing, you're not alone. I reviewed the report several times and through multiple filters, and while I respect the effort as one of the most honest profiles I've read from the FBI BSU, my heart is still unsettled.

While understandably frustrated, the FBI has respected public safety, your safety, by honoring the twelfth concept of predictable harm. They have, illustrated by the demanding work and difficult reporting, shared what they know, which is over one-half of the cases were preventable. In the end, the FBI has followed the advice and sent a heartfelt message to each of us in modeling Concept #12:

Don't Insist on Proof When You Have Enough Information to Prevent Harm:

As we know from recent events, active shootings continue to change our nation. The FBI is trying to educate us, hoping that the information contained in this study will help in efforts to promote safety across all communities. The initiative is appreciated; however, we must recognize a disturbing fact: Over one-half of these mass homicides involved threats and predictive behaviors, and those who knew of a direct-threat, including threats to kill, did not share what they knew until after the mass-slaughter of innocent parties.

While Kamikaze Pilots were specific to Japan, Suicide Bombers specific to the Middle-East, the Active-Shooter is very much an American phenomenon. We are better than this. We can be a better community-family, and we can certainly raise the bar in our care for one another. I suggest we pocket the blame and work toward a solution. I'm in, are you?

End of Chapter Nine

This concludes the main text. The remaining pages include multiple case studies; Accidents and Acts of Violence providing an opportunity to strengthen our predictive prowess with five strategic questions.

Thank you for your interest and the admiration you have for others and yourself. By working together, solutions are within reach. Feel free to contact my representative or me directly with questions, training requests, and to inquire about Keynote Presentations. I customize and facilitate presentations based on client-need; however, the website may offer a few thought-starters (soundpredictions.com). I respond to all requests within 48 hours.

Safe travels and thank you!,

Marcus

Mark (Marcus) Mann, Principal,
Soundpredictions.com
(206) 501-9170 (Voicemail or Text)
marcus@soundpredictions.com

Next, CASE STUDIES:

Case Studies

Don't forget to take advantage of the online risk assessment. The findings are available to you, and you alone.

MyRiskChecklist.com

Thank you!

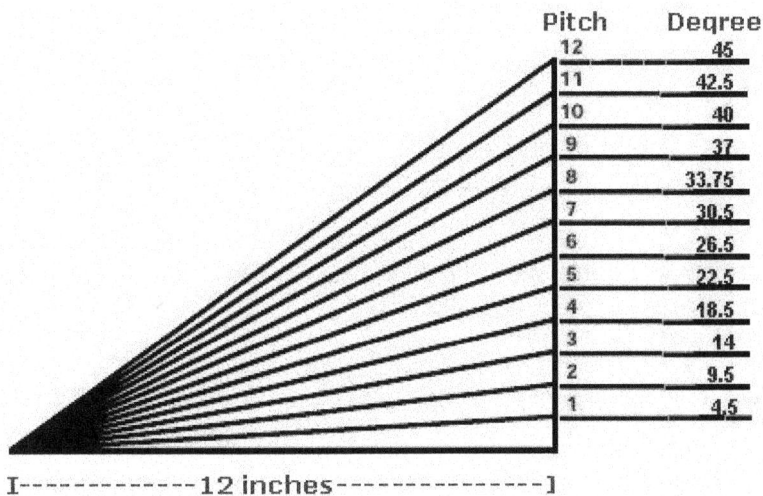

INCIDENT & ANALYSIS #1

Accidental Harm: Fatal Fall, Construction, Private Home, North Carolina

Contribution: NIOSH

This summary involves the tragic death of a 37-year-old laborer that fell approximately 13.5 feet from a residential roof to a concrete driveway; he died at once from his injuries. The laborer was working with a crew of eight workers for a construction subcontractor replacing shingles on a roof accessed by a ladder.

At the time of the incident, five workers were on the roof, including the laborer who was out of sight of his coworkers working on the garage side of the home. When the incident occurred, the coworkers heard the laborer hit the ground, rushed to his aid, and called 911. The laborer was pronounced dead at the scene.

1. Was it predictable? Yes.

2. What was the distraction? The employees (roofing labor) were well trained in how to harness and deploy fall protection; however,

questionably trained in checking the anchor point (the item selected for connection) and likely not trained in recalibrating to roof pitch.

3. Does it call for conversation, intervention or penalty? Yes. Anchor point selection and testing; a refresher on roof pitch.

4. Is the cause trending? Yes, a frequent accident with multiple causes.

5. What is the teachable resolution or short-term fix? The safety guidelines and written policy in this case were solid, if taught in their entirety and including a complete delivery … in the language of the employees. This crew had a clear and comprehensive safety program in the English language, but some didn't speak or read English, including the deceased. A quick fix includes five areas, all simple:

a. Have key safety guidelines printed and presented in both the primary and second language of the jobsite. Remember to confirm literacy (ask the employee face to face). Be honest about why you need to confirm literacy and language. Feel free to use this story as your rationale.

b. Shift or transfer safety orientation from the corporate office to the supervisor on-site or consider doing it at both locations.

c. Remind employees that 13 feet is a short walk, but a long fall; familiarity is a killer, time on the job numbs the risk, and we all need a reminder. Plus, that 15' foot retractable line looks good to visiting inspectors while offering nothing in a 13' fall. Feel free to use this story as your rationale for a refresher.

d. Constants Aren't: The anchor point may seem reliable, based on recent connections (tie-off) to seemingly reliable anchors. New anchor points are not always safe anchorage. That brick chimney used as last week's anchorage may not be a safe tie-off at a new job site.

e. A minor change in roof pitch needs re-calibration of the internal system (inner-ear) and a strong verbal reminder. Example: If employees are accustomed to working on a roof with a six-pitch (26-degree slope), a new pitch equates to a new job condition or new risk. Changing to a ten-pitch roof (40-degree slope) leads to trips, scuffs, and falls, even the ugly and instant fatality.

Note: If we understand the risk in changing work conditions, and we do not inform others, we can predict the harm. When we understand the need to familiarize employees to a change in working conditions, but do not supply the orientation, we can predict future harm.

NOTES

INCIDENT & ANALYSIS #2

Accidental Harm: Fatal Vehicle Accident, Construction, Tennessee

Contribution: Tennessee Public Safety Organizations

This backing accident involved a 28-year-old male laborer (the victim) died following injuries he received when a water truck drifted downhill and pinned him against a retaining wall he was washing.

The operator, working for the same employer, had parked the water truck on an incline on the entrance road, placed it into neutral, engaged the parking brake, and left it idling. Approximately 20 minutes later, the truck started drifting down the road as the victim washed the wall with his back to the water truck. The operator yelled to warn the victim, as he and a subcontractor ran behind the truck. The victim froze, and the water truck struck him, pinning him between the water truck and the wall. The operator backed the truck off the victim and called 911 on his mobile telephone as he checked the victim for injuries.

Emergency Medical Services (EMS), the county sheriff and fire department were dispatched to the incident arriving minutes later. EMS assessed the victim and found that he was having difficulty breathing. A life flight helicopter was requested, and the victim was transported to a state hospital where he was admitted and died two days later.

1. Was it predictable? Yes.

2. What was the distraction? Tombstone courage and the small size of the company brought down the bar; safety was not a priority due to the attitude 'too small for a big problem.' This was also illustrated by the lack of any written safety plan or policies, wheel chocks, reflective gear, and no continuous communication regarding safety fundamentals.

3. Does it call for conversation, intervention or penalty? A penalty after a fatality leaves a bad taste in my mouth, but this case certainly screams for the highest level of direct intervention, which is a penalty. The company failed to follow the most fundamental rules honoring human life, throwing common sense to the wind. What conversation could we possibly have about owners with low to no safety sense; not a simple error but multiple failures? I would be remiss to call this case a frequent-flyer; however, it deserves our attention.

4. Is the cause trending? No. This case involves a unique set of negligent behaviors, once compiled, are nothing less than criminal recklessness.

5. What is the teachable resolution or short-term fix? Where should we begin? A. We should ensure all equipment is inspected daily, and defective equipment is reported and removed from service. I differ from standard expectations regarding systems and equipment that could kill when they fail; operable condition is not the proper standard. The 'best condition' is the only acceptable standard when lives rely on it. The short-term fix includes increasing your expectations during inspections. The employer did not require the

water truck involved in this incident to be inspected prior to each shift. The water truck was equipped with a parking brake which was not inspected for full working load. It worked but did not work well. The lesson, brake test under full load.

B. We should designate a supervisor and/or a competent persona to be responsible for pre-shift equipment checks (every shift) and for verifying that any problems identified are corrected. Of course, we should have a safety policy and goal before we assign a responsible persona.

C. Deadline equipment (stop all use) when it does not meet 'best standards.' A requirement that all motor vehicles and other life sustaining equipment be removed from service until the repairs are made often works well, once the initial pain passes. Once implemented and consistently followed, we leverage the resources keeping productivity high and casualties low.

D. Employers should ensure that wheels are properly chocked on all vehicles, always, when they are parked or left unattended, on an incline, or not on a hill. According to the victim's employer, wheel chocks were purchased following this incident.

E. Training in recognizing and avoiding hazards should be given to all workers, coupled with employer assessments that workers are competent in predictable harm.

Note: If equipment is needed and requested, but never furnished, we can predict the harm. If needed equipment is purchased, issued, and not used, it is predictable harm.

M.K. Mann   SoundPredictions.com

NOTES:

Confidential On-line Assessment   MyRiskChecklist.com

INCIDENT & ANALYSIS #3

Intentional Harm: Mass Shooting, Public Venue, Las Vegas, Nevada

Contribution: FEMA

The Route 91 Harvest Festival is one of approximately 21,300 events and conventions that take place in Las Vegas per year. In 2017, 6,646,200 people attended conventions in Las Vegas.1 The Route 91 Harvest Festival is a country music festival organized annually since 2014 and staged at the Las Vegas Village concert venue in Las Vegas, Nevada. Route 91's approximately 17.5-acre venue plot is assembled directly across from the Mandalay Bay and the Luxor Hotel & Casino and is one of two open-air venues on the Las Vegas Strip. The fourth annual Route 91 concert series was held between September 29, 2017 and October 1, 2017.

On the third and final night of the festival, a lone gunman opened fire into the crowd from the 32nd floor of the Mandalay Bay Resort and Casino. The gunfire continued for over ten minutes, resulting in the deaths of 58 people and injuring more than 850, including first responders. Two local police officers responding to the incident were among those wounded by gunfire.

As the shooter engaged in this horrific act of mass violence, first responders made quick decisions, acting with bravery and professionalism to secure the scene and save lives. The cooperation between local fire departments, law enforcement agencies, and local private ambulance companies at the scene was exceptional. Off-duty public safety personnel also assisted in the response, providing valuable surge support for local responders. The Las Vegas community came together in response to this unprecedented situation to assist the survivors and responders of the shooting.

In the wake of this incident, it is important to evaluate the strengths and areas for improvement observed during the response—both to enhance the internal response capabilities of the Clark County Fire Department (CCFD) and the Las Vegas Metropolitan Police Department (LVMPD), as well as to share the knowledge gained from this incident with public safety agencies from across the country to assist in their preparedness efforts.

The Offender:
Stephen Paddock, Adult, No Prior Criminal Record.

The perpetrator of the shooting, Stephen Paddock, was born in Clinton, Iowa in 1953. His father, Benjamin Hoskins Paddock, was a convicted bank robber who escaped prison and was considered one of the FBI's most wanted in 1969. In 1977, Stephen Paddock received a degree in business administration from California State University, Northridge. He then worked as a government employee for the U.S. Postal Service and the Internal Revenue Service. Later, Paddock worked as an internal auditor for a company, which later became the defense contractor
Lockheed Martin, and then in the real estate business. Paddock did not have any criminal record prior to the shooting, save receiving a minor traffic citation, and had no known military
experience. In 2016, Paddock moved to Mesquite, Nevada located approximately 80 miles northeast of Las Vegas. Paddock lived in a

home with his girlfriend for several years. Residents of the community claimed Paddock was a private individual who deliberately kept a low profile.

Paddock gambled regularly and frequented casinos in Las Vegas, including the Mandalay Bay, which he would visit as often as twice a month. Six days prior to the shooting, Paddock checked into the Mandalay Bay, staying in a room on the 32nd floor. Paddock, unbeknownst to his neighbors and family members, legally and discreetly amassed an arsenal of weaponry, 33 items of which he acquired in the year prior to the incident. Law enforcement would discover 23 firearms inside Paddock's Mandalay Bay corner suite, which overlooked the Route 91 Harvest Festival

Actual Violence Timeframe: 10:05 PM – 10:15 PM **(Active Shooting 10 minutes)**

Incident Timeline:

October 1, 2017

9:40 PM Jason Aldean begins his performance on the Main Stage at the Route 91 Harvest Festival.

10:05 PM Paddock fires his first shots into the Las Vegas Village area from his room on the 32nd floor of Mandalay Bay.

10:06 PM Dispatch receives the first radio traffic from an officer and phone call from a civilian referencing the incident.

10:11 PM LVPD officers arrive on the 31st floor along with armed Mandalay Bay security officers.

10:13 PM CCFD Battalion 2 establishes Incident Command on Las

Vegas Boulevard.

10:15 PM Paddock fires his last shots into the Las Vegas Village area.

10:16 PM Paddock shoots himself between 10:16 and 10:18 PM.

10:17 PM First responding officers arrive on the 32nd floor of Mandalay Bay.

10:18 PM Officers contact a wounded security guard and cover down on Paddock's hallway.

10:18 PM CCFD T11 establishes a triage area and is assigned South Division at Russell and Las Vegas Boulevard South (LVBS). Patients begin arriving in the South via private vehicles.

10:22 PM CCFD E11 establishes a triage area and is assigned North Division at Tropicana and Koval Street.

10:23 PM Additional officers arrive on the 32nd floor of Mandalay Bay.

10:24 PM CCFD E18 sets up a triage, treatment, and transport area at Tropicana and LVBS with E33 and R33.

10:26 PM Additional officers arrive on the 32nd floor of Mandalay Bay.

10:26 PM Unified Command is established at South Central Area Command.

10:35 PM The Clark County Multi-Agency Coordination Center and the LVPD Department Operations Center are established.

10:40 PM Distraction Call #1: There is a person wearing fatigues entering an RV at Tropicana and Koval.

10:41 PM A Strike Team ascends the stairs from the 30th floor and clears the 31st floor.

10:56 PM The Strike Team reenters the stairwell from the 31st floor and walks up to the 32nd floor.

10:56 PM CCFD C2 establishes a triage area and is assigned East Division. This triage area is located on the east side of the venue on Giles near gate 4A.

11:01 PM The first CCFD Rescue Task Force is assigned to enter the Route 91 venue.

11:20 PM The Strike Team conducts an explosive breach into room 32-135 and makes entry. The team reports that Paddock is down from an apparent self-inflicted gunshot wound.

1. Was it predictable? Possibly.

2. What was the distraction? High density casino activity 24/7, elusive and alienated offender, tolerance, privacy, and fear of judging the offender. Paddock declined maid services for multiple days in a row, while amassing 33 firearms in a single suite; this was a deviation from the norm; however, not the policy of Mandalay Bay or other large casino lodging facility.

3. Does it call for conversation, intervention or penalty? Yes. Conversation regarding the misapplication of tolerance, avoidance, and fear of judging the offender and his behaviors. This offender displayed escalating aggression hidden by frequent geographical and employment changes. While the single purchase of a firearm is

routine, amassing 30 firearms is atypical, a big red flag.

4. Is the cause trending? Yes. The speed of interagency communication remains flawed; defending existing lines over improvement is the norm. Broken communication in the private sector contributes, other influential groups should examine process and procedures remains flawed.

5. What is the teachable resolution or short-term fix? Declining maid services for nearly a week is an easy fix; the two-day rule would have possibly interrupted Paddock's rage cycle. This was not the policy of Mandalay Bay or the policy was not asserted. This incident provides another example supporting use of existing laws tracking multiple purchases of firearms. Providing a possible clue, and a deviation from the norm; both amassing firearms and isolating in a licensed business for nearly a week can be addressed by policy or use of existing law.

Also, the importance of coordinated planning across agencies cannot be understated in terms of its impact on this response. When agencies followed pre-established plans and procedures, they improved communication and strengthened the response. Where plans were not integrated or not widely known and understood by responders across all responding agencies, difficulties arose. Strengthening plans, policies, and procedures across Southern Nevada public safety agencies will reinforce their capabilities, allowing them to respond as effectively as possible in future emergencies.

Note: If we understand the need for coordinated training, and fail to coordinate training, we can predict the harm. If we understand the destructive nature of secrecy and allow a man to isolate on our property for a week, we can predict the harm.

NOTES:

NOTES:

INCIDENT & ANALYSIS #4

Accidental Harm: Fatal Swimming Pool Maintenance Incident, San Diego, California

Contribution: OSHA

This case involves an assistant pool manager electrocuted when she contacted an ungrounded electric motor. She was performing her work duty of maintaining the pH level of the swimming pool. Her duties included removing the power from the electric motor, checking the chemical standards of the water, and adding soda ash to the water as needed.

Standing barefoot on the wet concrete floor of the pump room, she filled a plastic drum with water, plugged in the mixing motor and placed the motor switch in the on position. In the process of adding soda ash to the water-filled drum, she accidentally contacted the energized mixing motor with her left hand and created a path to ground for the electrical current. She was electrocuted and died. She was 17.

1. Was it predictable? Yes.

2. What was the distraction? Not applicable.

3. Does it call for conversation, intervention or penalty? Yes. Those who maintain the equipment should be involved in the inspection of, training for use, and supervision for first-time users. None of the above were in-play at the time of this senseless tragedy.

4. Is the cause trending? No.

5. What is the teachable resolution or short-term fix? Training is the short-term fix; working out the bare-basics of electricity and safety would be a good start. I would suggest training at the top-level first, followed by mid-management and line-level, all on the same day. Next, maintain all equipment, routinely inspect and repair or replace equipment that is faulty, damaged or presents a safety hazard.

In this case, the mixing motor was in poor condition with a faulty electrical ground. An electrical supply cord with the grounding pin intact may have prevented this fatality. Also, the ground-fault circuit interrupters (GFCIs) in this case, were not properly wired or functioning, and would have de-energized the circuit, thereby preventing the fatality.

Most know that electrical equipment should not be installed in rooms that do not have adequate drainage to prevent water accumulation during normal operation or filter maintenance. But do we breach that duty-owed when we expect a temporary, teen-worker to have the same level of knowledge?

The employer should have ensured adequate drainage of the pump room to avoid water accumulating on the floor and contributing to the electrocution hazard. Also, all employees entering the pump room should wear insulated boots/shoes. Had the floor been dry and had the victim been wearing insulated boots or shoes, this fatality might have been prevented. But should an unsupervised 17-year-old be expected to know all-of-the-above? Once again, someone supervising the young employee had a duty-owed to do more. Even if the victim did know of the risk, which it appears she did not, this was predictable harm.

If you've ever wondered why 'everyone' gets training when one or two people have errored, this case provides a good example. Certain injuries, blamed on the individual or others, often expose unknown cultural problems. The Culture of Assumptions is common, and in this case, assumptions were off-the-charts; the belief that all 'must know' the basics of electricity and water led to fatality. If a casualty occurs and the culture is a mystery, I suggest everyone receives training or re-training. In nearly every Culture of Assumptions they have not trained together, ended crucial orientation training for new employees, or suspended training altogether. In the end, they have no known or very little common knowledge or language.

Note: If you have ended crucial training programs, we can predict harm. If you have sought new employees, pay them less so you can avoid training, the harm is predictable.

NOTES:

NOTES:

INCIDENT & ANALYSIS #5

Intentional Harm: Former Employee, Fatal Shooting Post-Termination, New York

Contribution: Confidential Client

This case involves an ongoing dispute (employee on employee), and fits the escalating pattern mentioned throughout the book. The two employees had an ongoing verbal dispute, which was protracted, visible, and at one point involved physical contact and assault. Eventually, the employer terminated one employee for conduct violating both policy and NY laws.

The violence was the peak of increasing strain between co-workers, anger toward one another leading to both men filing police reports. The terminated employee, who was not provided with an exit interview, made additional threats prior to exiting for what the employer erroneously believed was the final goodbye. The offender returned and killed the victim-employee as the worker followed his regular routine, exiting work in the usual manner, with a horrific and outcome. The victim was pronounced dead at the scene.

1. Was it predictable? Yes, absolutely.

2. What was the distraction? Denial, ignorance, and possibly a heavy workload. This company was very busy; a frequent-flyer when good

people rush a risky process. I see this tragic formula far too often; a case in need of strategic contemplation yet rushed because we don't have the time.

3. Does it call for conversation, intervention or penalty? Yes, conversation with a dash of training intervention. This case should have never ended with additional violence. Escalation-flags consisted of A) a reoccurring conflict, which continued after employer intervention, B) physical contact between two employees, which should trigger an immediate suspension-with-pay for both, and C) law enforcement involvement without arrest, a risk factor which surprises most employers. As a conflict escalates, police may be called as part of a healthy response; however, we should watch for a spike in escalation when no enforcement action is taken. One of many reasons we send the combatants home with pay for a 72-hour cool-down.

4. Is the cause trending? This case represents a frequent-flyer; it's a common-conflict scenario that usually does not end in violence, and typically involves thoughts of violence on the part of both employees. Determined after multiple interviews, violent thoughts are typical, specifically, within the male species, and after conventional solutions appear to have failed. Energy Follows Thought! Once the thought of violence is in the mind, actual violence is one step away.

5. What is the teachable resolution or short-term fix? Suspend with pay and do it proudly. Once it escalates, we should shift our thinking from individual employee rights to workplace violence reduction. The behavior, not HR or the boss, triggers the protection of all employees. Second, while we'll never know, a formal exit interview may have de-escalated the offender. Also, risk escalates in the case of mutual combatants; once we sanction one employee while taking no action against the other. Facts are not relevant at this point as emotion runs high, and reasoning often drops to an all-time low.

No Further Harm: A Purely Predictable Path

NOTES:

NOTES:

INCIDENT & ANALYSIS #6

Intentional Harm: Disgruntled Reader, Topic of a News Story, Mass Shooting, Fatal, Maryland

Contributions: Client / Public Domain:

This case involves an active shooter with a long and destructive memory. The mass shooting occurred at the offices of The Capital, a newspaper serving Annapolis, Maryland. The gunman shot and killed five employees in 2018 with a shotgun, while others were injured trying to escape. The gunman was arrested while hiding under a desk at the crime scene and is currently imprisoned.

The victims were selected randomly based on opportunity / proximity, and all worked for The Capital newspaper in Annapolis. The victims were exclusively newsroom employees for the publication, which published an article in 2011 about the offender. He had been placed on probation for harassing an acquaintance from high school through social media and email. The offender, enraged by the article, brought a defamation lawsuit against The Capital. A judge later dismissed the suit, creating a secondary rage point. The offender then started sending messages to the newspaper expressing his wrath; letters, emails, and voice messages included threats to attack their office and staff. To diffuse the offender, the newspaper ignored threats, And took no legal action against the offender.

Enraged by their silence, he travelled to the newspaper's main office, barricaded the rear door, shot through the glass of a secure front entrance, entered and committed the acts of violence.

1. Was it predictable? Yes, with a qualification.

2. What was the distraction? Denial and tombstone courage due to the frequency of past threats and institutionalized comfort with dissatisfied customers or readers. Danger was minimized due to a false belief that the offender, with a pattern of multiple threats without actual violence, would continue in the same rage design.

3. Does it call for conversation, intervention or penalty? The penalty has been exercised in the form of a criminal sentence, the opportunity for intervention was missed, and conversation is a must. This is a difficult case when it comes to prevention; the occupation of news reporting, much like nursing, the IRS, and policing, requires a thick skin. That tough flesh that protects the spirit also acts as a barrier to predictable clues. Negativity and complaints are the norm at any news organization, a possible set-up in minimizing bona fide threats of violence.

4. Is the cause trending? Yes, part of an increase or a violent phase, which began in late 2016 and exploded in 2017.

5. What is the teachable resolution or short-term fix? When a threat is made, we must take it seriously. Implied threats are difficult; however, direct threats must be taken seriously every time. Predictable violence has only a few rules. Responding seriously and promptly to all threats is crucial. Clients and students often ask me how to assess threats of harm. My short answer, if someone says they are going to hurt you, believe them. The rule holds true whether the threat is made by a teen, person, or a global terrorist; if they say they intend to harm you or your colleagues, believe them.

NOTES:

NOTES:

No Further Harm: A Purely Predictable Path

INCIDENT & ANALYSIS #7

Accidental Harm: 747 Airliner, Math Mistake, Manitoba, Canada

Contribution: NTSB:

This case is crowded with fatal assumptions, courage under stress, lessons, and a happy ending. This scenario also offers one of the finest examples of an innocent error creating major loss potential. It begins with a routine flight involving a brand-new Boeing 767, and two experienced pilots assigned to the daily Montreal-Ottawa-Edmonton route. Prior to take off, the pilots reported 69 souls onboard.

The plane was cruising at an altitude of 41,000 feet when the engines abruptly started losing power. Then one of the jet engines shut down completely, which is not a problem, until  other engines do the same. They did. The pilots skimmed their checklists and attempted several re-starts without success. With no engines the 767 became a 395,000-pound object falling from the sky; a glider at best, and most likely a mass casualty. Industry insiders call this rare scenario a "dead-stick" flight, and a dead-stick landing in a commercial jetliner is nearly always fatal. The pilots had no other option; they dedicated precious time to calculating the drop, the glide, and where that might end, hopefully a landing rather than a crash.

In the end, the stars were aligned for this crew and their terrified passengers. They recalled an old military runway named Gimli; a closed airstrip now used for drag-racing. Ironically, one pilot used to land his glider on this very strip, and he was about to do it again in a 767. They landed safely, while over the recommended speed, on a very short runway, and with no flaps or engine power. In the end the damage was comparatively minor, and 69 survivors were elated.

The captain, Robert Pearson, was helped in gauging his approach to the 6,800-foot-long strip by the fact that he had had a glider-pilot license for 10 years. Another fortunate circumstance was that the copilot, Maurice Quintal, had taken training in the Canadian Air Force at the Gimli field, which is no longer in active use except as a drag strip for automobile races

Once the applause died down, they investigated the cause of complete engine failure, and found it equally shocking. Prior to the first leg of the journey, the aircraft received standard care and fuel from the ground crew. The crew loved the new 767-233; Canada's first metric aircraft, which called for a new fueling formula, a conversion from standard to metric units of fuel. The conversion factors were not used, and the error quietly slipped by. The net result led the pilots to believe the figure for fuel weight was in kilograms when it had been pumped using a measurement of pounds. Since one kilogram equals 2.2 pounds, the plane took off with half the fuel that it should have had. The 767 simply ran out of gas at 41,000 feet.

1. Was it predictable? Yes, while perfectly understandable, the 767-Gimli incident involved foreseeable harm. The metric conversion is only one example of many new standards or so-called little things

that shield us from significant consequences. When we expose the predictable elements missed, we identify the training need.

2. What was the distraction? Assumptions, minimizing, and failure to train or communicate are considered distractions under this plan; people knew and missed something due to a distraction. Uncover the distraction and you have exposed the lifesaving policy or action-step needed.

In the 767-Gimli incident the ground crew and flight deck did not give the new conversion formula the weight it deserved. After all, it was a small change; so small, everyone gets it. Most leaders and organizations would treat a simple mathematical change similarly, and employees follow their lead. Motivation is contagious; changes downplayed by the boss or safety lead often receive a lukewarm response from employees. Delivering little changes with little energy often meet the same level of enthusiasm by employees. While results are rarely this dramatic, minimizing the details of a crucial safety strategy because it seems simple is a common and honest mistake. The metric conversion related to the Canadian Airline was discussed but not treated as a core safety issue. Unfortunately, it wouldn't be the last example.

3. Does the injury, loss, or near-miss call for conversation, intervention, penalty? The near-miss, significant property damage and non-injurious events, usher in the ideal opportunity for leadership at any level. In most cases, a conversation is first, followed by a decision for intervention (a defined and documented change), or a penalty (discipline, mandatory training, plus some).

Lessons are plentiful in every crisis, but the near-miss provides an opportunity for conversation minus the tears. The conversion glitch is only the icon, a vote supporting those who campaign for unconventional details shared promptly, and in some cases globally.

The Gimli Glider event could be any near miss of any size supporting a need for communication and the importance of sharing data beyond the confines of a single organization. There's no need to wait until it hits home, you can use the five questions to assess any incident regardless of your involvement.

4. Is the cause trending? Trending is too harsh a term for the Gimli affair; however, patterns aren't necessary when examining such a large incident or a threat that may be expanding. Trending simply calls for urgency, communication, and shared-lessons beyond the company or community property lines. Trending typically signals an uncomfortable share to prevent further harm. The timeliness of shared data after the unexpected 767 landing at Gimli was excellent. We also know it happened again, a conversion error on a grander financial scale; brilliant people had missed the error until a devastating loss forced the full review of a 125-million-dollar mistake.

In this case, a satellite was supposed to be the first weather observer in a foreign atmosphere. But as it approached the red planet to slip into a stable path, the pride of NASA vanished. In the final moments of life, the orbiter shared her story; sending data indicating a dip dangerously low into the Martian atmosphere. The orbiter followed her program and continued a tad too far, too fast, and too hot for survival. The NASA review board found that the software calculated for a light entry into the Mars atmosphere had missed the mark. Like errors of the recent past, the orbiter satellite was set to thrust pounds of force, while other software settings assumed Metric Units. The NASA Orbiter burned to death due to a conversion error.

5. What is the solution or a short-term fix? You might be considering conventional takeaways; the need to check, double-check, and triple-check calculations. The lesson goes beyond confirming the numbers. Boeing, NASA, and Canadian air crash investigators were pioneers in transparency. The short-term fix is the same in workplace violence

and other injuries; communicate quickly and broadly to help others avoid the same circumstances.

NOTES:

M.K. Mann   SoundPredictions.com

NOTES:

INCIDENT & ANALYSIS #8

Accidental Harm: Natural Gas Explosion, Fatal, Failure to Evacuate, Canton, Illinois

Contribution: NTSB

On November 16, 2016, about 5:44 p.m., a natural gas-fueled explosion occurred at a two-level commercial building located in Canton, Illinois. One employee was killed, and 11 people were injured. Prior to the accident, a sub-contractor for the main communications company was performing directional drilling adjacent to the victim-building. They were preparing to install conduit for a fiber optic cable. The subcontractor began performing multiple drills at various locations on the block. At 3:58 p.m., the contractor reported a gas line had been damaged. The damage occurred while crews were pulling the drill rod back to the drilling rig after a directional path was completed under the sidewalk.

At 4:06 p.m., the owner and operator of the gas line, received the damage report and dispatched field technicians to evaluate the situation. About 7 minutes later, the first responder arrived at the scene; three other technicians arrived shortly thereafter. The lead responder contacted his supervisor, confirmed the pipeline had been struck, and requested excavation equipment to uncover the line. A backhoe excavator arrived at 4:41p.m. and technicians began to isolate the leak.

At 4:48 p.m., nearby customers called the Natural Gas Customer Contact Center to report natural gas odors both indoors and outdoors. Any customers and complainants that called in were given safety instructions and told to leave their building if an odor was detected. By 5:37 p.m., technicians shut off the natural gas flow to the service line by squeezing off the pipeline. Seven minutes later, at 5:44 p.m., the Opera House Annex (victim building identified earlier) exploded, killing one and injuring 11 who were impacted by debris from the blast.

1. Was it predictable? Yes, no qualifications or training made this accident predictable. Plus, the day of the accident was the first field work day for the employee-in-charge (crew leader) of the directional drilling crew.

2. What was the distraction? Tombstone Courage: failure to respect published requirements, prequalification, and therefore, unable to understand the risk and the need for planning.

3. Does it call for conversation, intervention or penalty? This calls for more than a conversation or intervention; no written project plan, no emergency response plans for the job, and workers without qualifications or training call for serious penalties.

4. Is the cause trending? No.

5. What is the teachable resolution or short-term fix? This scenario calls for a toast to basic safety protocols. Minimal standards could have prevented this tragedy; taking advantage of time after the first external clue could have prevented all casualties.

The gas line was damaged at 3:58 p.m., private parties on-site continued to complain about the odor at 4:48 p.m., and the blast occurred at 5:44 p.m. The crews attended to several urgencies for over ninety minutes; however, 9-1-1 was not called and formal evacuation was never executed; both would have likely prevented further harm.

NOTES:

About the Author

Mark (Marcus) Mann is a professional facilitator, leadership instructor, and recognized crisis negotiator. As Principal for Sound Predictions LLC, he's known for high-energy, humorous delivery, and pragmatic advice. He facilitates a strategy for lasting change, problem-solving, and the rapid exchange of knowledge. He's recognized for unconventional employee development, leadership coaching, and well-known for leading crucial conversations with respect. Beyond his day-to-day duties, he also provides support in the form of legislative and courtroom testimony.

Prior to the private sector, Marcus served 22 years in military service, public safety, and community leadership. He was responsible for the Hostage Negotiations Unit, Critical Incident Stress Management Team, and the Training Unit. Marcus also served the Risk Review & Reduction Process for several organizations recognizing patterns, developing strategies, and ethical training and coaching solutions. This is his third book. Predictable (previously featured by Pearson Custom, released by reversion 2017), now available on Amazon and Kindle, publication date February 25, 2019.

Mark Mann attended the University of Virginia (Quantico), graduating from the FBI National Academy (Session 211). His training-track included behavioral science, employment law, and performance art. He is an active volunteer, currently serving Boots to Shoes; War Veteran Transitions. For recreation, he hikes the trails of the great northwest and may be heard cursing a sand trap while golfing near his Camano Island home. He shares his motivation for teaching, influence, and problem-solving in one simple and sound prediction: **"First, we change what they know. They often change what they do."**

Legal Disclaimer (full version)

This text, introductory proposals, previously presented training sessions in the public and private sectors, focus groups, and commercial for-profit instruction. This disclaimer covers a compilation written by Mark Kevin Mann, AKA Marcus Mann, dba Sound Predictions, a Limited Liability Corporation, established in 2004, 2011, and in good standing at the time of this publication. The protected entity and all intellectual property rights originate and remain with the Principal of Sound Predictions, M. K. Mann, Stanwood, Washington, 98292. Protections include:

1. Original release, collegiate text: Anti-Terrorism Risk Assessments, Published by Pearson Custom Publishing, 2005. Reversion of Copyright initiated by the author and approved in contractual format by Pearson. Reversion includes all rights after acknowledgement of Pearson Publishing; granted the author on February 8, 2017.

2. No Further Harm Pilot: Clues, Concepts & Cues of Danger (Short Form and Predictability Risk Checklist), supplemental information in short form, published by the author, up to January 25, 2019.

3. No Further Harm: (full text), includes this book, all information in long form, posters, social media posts, guest media, and articles published by the author, up to, on, and after January 25, 2019. All rights reserved; specific permission is required from the author if reprinted, quoted, cited in any form, shared electronically or otherwise transferred. For educational purposes, the versions mentioned above include specific context and unique instructional styles; sequence, titles, and original verbiage, including the Respect-Respond-Review process, which remain protected by trademark and copyright; explicit permission required from the author if reprinted, quoted in unrelated publications shared electronically or otherwise assigned. or repeated in any form.

Understanding risky behavior, accidents, potential offenders, and the reduction of dangerous habits include both natural laws and changing science. This book provides information deemed reliable at the time of publication. The publisher and author share intellectual property with a warning; lowering risk is possible, and eliminating risk is not. Furthermore, this text does not replace the law; employment contracts, policy, collective bargaining agreements, and common sense, which must be considered side-by-side with the cues and clues of risk contained in this text. Liability for damage shifts to the consumer when any theory from this publication is shared with permission or applied. We rely on the reader to use common sense and consider the context for predicting and responding to perceived hazards.

All trademarks, registered trademarks, and registered service marks are the property of their respective owners and are used herein for identification purposes; Pearson Custom Publishing, CCI, and the Library of Congress, United States of America, printed and electronically registered in 2005, 2016, and 2019. Questions and permission may be satisfied by contacting the author or author's representative online:

Soundpredictions.com,
Personal Risk Checklist: myriskchecklist.com,
marcus@soundpredictions.com,
or direct (206) 501-9170 (Pacific Standard Time).

www.ingramcontent.com/pod-product-compliance
Lightning Source LLC
Chambersburg PA
CBHW061635040426
42446CB00010B/1423